Between THIMBLE & THUMB

Between THIMBLE & THUMB

by
Shirley J. Botsford

DRAWINGS BY PATRICIA JEWEL WYNNE

Holt, Rinehart and Winston   New York

Published by Holt, Rinehart and Winston,
383 Madison Avenue, New York, New York 10017.

Published simultaneously in Canada by Holt, Rinehart and Winston of Canada, Limited.

Library of Congress Cataloging in Publication Data
Botsford, Shirley J.
Between thimble & thumb.

1. Sewing.   2. Needlework.   I. Title.
TT705.B67   746.4′4   78-16332
ISBN Hardbound: 0-03-017501-1
ISBN Paperback: 0-03-050546-1

Drawings by Patricia Jewel Wynne
Photographs by Roger Craig Merritt
Designer: Helen Barrow
Printed in the United States of America

10 9 8 7 6 5 4 3 2

Between Thimble & Thumb *is dedicated to Ruth Jean, who taught me how to do everything; to James Howard, who insisted that everything be done correctly; to Gary, because the only things that he ever liked about me were my quilts; to Craig, who always knew I could do it (and told me so when I didn't); to Pat Wynne, who illustrated every stitch as carefully as I sewed them; to Pam Hoffman, who was there no matter what the time, sewing and remaining calm in a crisis; to Kris Garmire, for her enthusiasm; to Ellyn Polshek, my editor, who is one of the most understanding people I know; and to Helen Barrow, a new friend.*

Contents

Introduction

My first sewing attempt was a quilt that measured 4" x 6" and fit the bed of my favorite doll. It was made from scraps of fabric that I rescued from the waste basket in my mother's sewing room. I was as proud of that tiny quilt as my grandmother must have been of her very best one.

Since then, sewing has become my career as well as my favorite pastime. Still, I occasionally take out that first effort and think of how meaningful it was to me.

Although a quilt is practical on a cold winter's night, it must now also be unique to the taste and lifestyle of its owner. It is no longer enough to be able to recognize a piece of your Dad's old shirt or your baby brother's pajamas.

Today, almost everyone wants their activities to reflect their own individuality. This is particularly evident in sewing.

A stitch in time still does save nine; however, noticeably less fine quality hand sewing is being done for the sake of practicality. It now fulfills a need for self expression.

Darning, mending, and patching have become enthusiastic, creative, and ingenious. Clothing frequently bears miniature art exhibits of embroidery and intricate patchwork.

Interest in the crafts is constantly becoming more evident. Crafts are a way for you to express yourself. You can make things that express your own unique personality. At the same time you can observe and experience the satisfaction of making something by hand in a leisurely, step-by-step, evolutionary process. As a result you will find that you will become well-versed in evaluating the quality of the craftsmanship of an object. You will learn to appreciate the finest work and probably become the most severe critic of your own work. Whether you are a stitcher or a collector, you are part of the new sewing circle.

A quilt may seem like an enormous undertaking that most people won't want to tackle as their first effort. However, the list of sewn projects that you can do is endless, everything from simple dinner napkins to complicated sleeping bags. Gifts are especially fun to make and personalize by sewing.

I decided to write this book to acquaint the beginner as well as the accomplished sewer with contemporary uses for old techniques.

This book demonstrates fourteen different sewing techniques and applies them to a variety of projects including a full-size quilt. The projects range from a sewing caddy made from layers of reverse appliquéd fabrics to a practical tote bag and a roomy duffle bag made from different styles of patchwork.

You do not need to have any previous sewing experience. The book gives you all the information that you need to know. Find some time and some space. Get together everything you need and plunge in!

The directions are presented in a very basic, step-by-step form. Suggestions and simplifications are given for the experienced and inexperienced. Certain steps can be eliminated for a more simplified project. Advanced sewers can expand the directions and use their own inventiveness to create a more intricate or decorative project. Each project will be unique and personal to you because of the choices you will make as you follow the instructions and suggestions.

Part I of the book, Beginning with Basics, contains seven chapters of information about tools and their use, important terms, and working methods that will be used frequently throughout the entire book. Read this section carefully before you begin working. Refer to it while you are sewing and whenever you have a question.

There are fourteen chapters in Part II, Sample Blocks and Projects to Make With Them. Each one is dedicated to a different sewing technique. Each one is complete, including lists of supplies, directions, and easy-to-follow illustrations.

The first section in each chapter demonstrates a particular technique by showing you how to make a 14" x 14" square sample piece that I will call a "block." The second part of the chapter gives instructions for incorporating the block into a practical project. Because these sample blocks are all the same size, they can be used to make any of the other projects in the book.

For example, Chapter One provides directions for making a 14" block of basic quilting. With this block, you can follow instructions in the second part of the chapter and construct a clever but simple apron.

The project in Chapter Two is a pillow made from a 14" block of colorful patchwork that you design yourself. The quilted block from Chapter One is interchangeable and can be used to make the pillow in Chapter Two if you wish to do so.

Each project can be completed with an infinite variety of fabrics and colors to reflect your own creativity and personal touch. Similiarly, the fourteen chapters contain fourteen blocks and fourteen projects that are interchangeable. Any one project can be made fourteen different ways. In fact, there are 196 variations you can make!

Many of the projects in the book are completed with only one block. There are five projects that require more than one block. These projects are mentioned below, with the number of blocks that are needed to complete them.

In Chapter Three, A Tag-along Tote uses two blocks. A Durable Duffle, the project in Chapter Four, takes four blocks. A Timeless Tablecloth in Chapter Seven is made with sixteen blocks. The Creative Café Curtains in Chapter Eight require the number of blocks needed to cover your window. A Questioning Quilt, Chapter Fourteen, is made from twelve different blocks.

Check the instructions for the project you intend to make before you begin making any blocks. Determine how many blocks are needed for the project, and be sure to buy enough supplies to make them all at one time. It is often impossible to match fabrics later if you run out.

At the end of each chapter are special sewing tips—Suggestions and Simplifications—for the beginner and the more accomplished sewer. Here you will find innovative ideas and some challenging recommendations for making each project more decorative or more personalized, plus ways to make each project faster and easier.

As you see your first accomplishment followed by another, you will look forward to finding out more and experimenting with the different techniques in each chapter. You will find that creating something with different fabrics and methods is both challenging and fun. The planning of each project, the selection of fabrics, and the experimenting with design and color can be the most exciting parts of the process.

It's really very simple if you relax, take lots of time, and follow the step-by-step instructions and illustrations carefully. By beginning slowly and methodically, you will be making and designing your own things sooner than you think.

By completing each chapter and interchanging the techniques with the different projects, you will develop your own special formula for creating and designing.

If you are just beginning to sew, I suggest that you start with Part One, Beginning with Basics, and work through the book in order. I do not repeat the explanation of any basic technique if it has been described in an earlier block or project or in Part I. When a basic technique is repeated, I will refer you to the block or project or place in Part I where it was demonstrated initially.

I hope you will look upon this book as a guideline that will challenge your creative spirits and encourage you to design things that demonstrate your own tastes and interests in fabric and the crafts.

Try to master the basic skills well so that your results are not spoiled by sloppiness. The best design can be ruined by bad technique. Learn from your mistakes, learn to be patient, and most of all don't be too hard on yourself!

Whether you are making something special for yourself, or a gift, or even something to keep in your family for generations, I hope Between Thimble & Thumb will provide you with ways to spend many wonderful hours and that you will enjoy the satisfaction that comes from making things yourself.

Part I

BEGINNING WITH BASICS

CHAPTER ONE

An Assortment of Time-saving Tools

You may want to add to the assortment of sewing supplies that you already have. Below is a list of equipment that you will use to complete the projects in this book. All of these supplies are necessary for working quickly and efficiently.

SUPPLIES TO HAVE ON HAND FOR ALL THE PROJECTS

Drawing Supplies:

1. cardboard
2. clear ruler
3. compass or circle template
4. erasers
5. masking tape
6. paper scissors
7. plain paper or pattern paper
8. soft pencils in black, pink, and white
9. tracing paper

Sewing Supplies:

1. cutting shears
2. embroidery scissors
3. hand sewing needles
4. iron
5. safety pins
6. sewing machine
7. straight pins
8. tape measure
9. thimble
10. thread in white and black

Most of these are used for every project. They will not be listed on the supplies list. Read through the instructions before starting a block or project to make sure you know what tools you will need.

Keep everything in a handy spot near your work area to save time and steps. Project 9 shows you how to make a nifty collapsible sewing box that hangs up while you are working. It folds up when you are finished and looks great.

A large, flat work area with good light is essential. It can be portable or temporary. A folding cardboard cutting board is perfect. You can find it in most notion departments. It can be used on a bed or dining room table and is easily stored when you are not using it.

If you don't have a special sewing room, you might commandeer a closet or corner in the bedroom just for your own work area. Wherever it is, make certain it's organized and cheery before you try to work there. Hang up an "Inspiration" board for your ideas, sketches, and clippings from magazines. Tack up swatches of fabric in colors that you love. You might like to put up a shelf, as a personal touch. Display a special collection of your favorite things; plants, dolls, shells, anything that you like. This will give you a source for ideas and color combinations as well as make your work space cozy. Change your miniature exhibitions every once in a while to give yourself a fresh outlook.

Choose your sewing supplies carefully. You will want to get tools that will serve the purpose and last long.

Visit the sewing notions departments in different stores. A good one will have a large selection of thread, buttons, zippers, trimmings, and elastic, as well as tools. Browse through the different sewing aids and read the instructions for their use. Be selective. Some of the new gadgets can save you time and improve your results tremendously. I confess to having a drawer full of "wonderful and amazing" sewing contraptions. Most of them do not work well and make an otherwise easy job *more* difficult to do.

Beeswax:

This is used to lightly coat the surface of your thread during hand sewing. It makes the thread stronger and more slippery. The surface of the thread is made smoother by the wax, and thus your thread will not snarl and knot frequently.

Beeswax is usually found in a plastic dispenser with comb-like teeth. Pull a length of thread through the teeth against the wax twice.

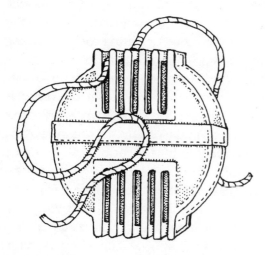

A beeswax dispenser showing thread pulling through the teeth

Hand Sewing Needles:

Needles come in a variety of styles and sizes. Some jobs may require a special needle. Get a package of needles that has a good selection of types and sizes. Experiment with the different ones to find the kind that is easiest for you to work with.

"Sharps" come in all sizes and do almost any job adequately. Generally, the finer the work, the finer the needle should be. If the needle is too large, it will be difficult to push through the fabric. If it is dull, it will make snags or ugly holes in the fabric.

Iron:

Preferably a good steam iron. Keep it clean and rust free. Empty and dry it after each use. This will prevent stains and brown rust marks from ruining your projects. Use distilled or purified water only.

L Square:

A lighter-weight or plastic version of a carpenter's square is called an L square. You will need to make perpendicular lines and right angles frequently. The L square makes drawing directly on the fabric fast and accurate. A T square or right triangle can be used for the same purpose.

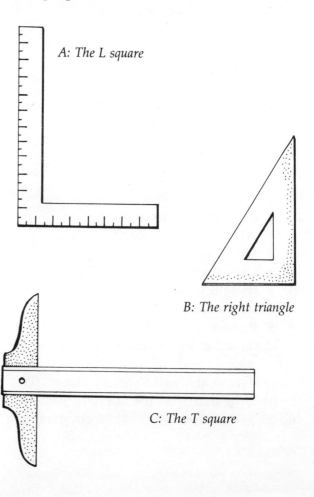

A: The L square

B: The right triangle

C: The T square

Machine Sewing Needles:

Machine needles come in different sizes and types. The needle that you select should correspond to the thread and the fabric in weight and type.

Size nine is the finest needle and is used for silk, chiffon, etcetera. Sizes eleven and fourteen are good for general sewing. Size eighteen is very heavy duty and is used for thick coat fabrics, canvas, etcetera. Use *only* the type of needles that are recommended for *your* machine. Check your sewing machine manual to make sure that you have the needle inserted properly and tightly.

One side of the needle has a long thread groove in it. This groove should be facing the direction from which you thread the needle.

The condition of the needle is important. Many of the problems and difficulties that occur during sewing can be blamed on a defective needle and not on you! Keep the needles sharp and free of oil. Examine the needle frequently and especially before beginning each new project. Change the needle if you notice any of the following defects:

1. Barbs at the point will cause snags and pulls in the fabric.
2. A dull or broken point will not penetrate the fabric and may cause tearing or holes in the fabric.
3. A bent needle will not allow the machine to function properly. It will only become more bent with use. It may hit the throat plate of the machine and break during sewing. This can be dangerous because the broken piece may fly up and hit you. I'm not suggesting that you wear goggles while sewing, merely that you don't try to use a bent needle for "just one more seam."
4. A scratched or damaged needle is difficult to use because it does not go through the layers of fabric easily. If the problem is minor, such as dirt, rust, or build-up of fabric finishes on the needle, you can correct it easily. Remove the needle and poke it through the emery bag attached to your pin cushion a few times. Test it in the machine to see if the problem stops. If this doesn't help, replace the needle with a new one. If the needle is badly scratched, it is abrasive to the thread. This causes constant breaking of the thread. Often only one fiber of the thread will break and you will continue sewing with only one-half of the fibers of the thread. The broken fiber will snag up in the machine and form a knot. Eventually it will break.

Machine needles are available with different types of points for use on special materials. Test your needle on a scrap of the fabric before beginning the project.

1. *Sharp point* needles are for all woven fabrics. They will sew a wide variety of materials well.
2. *Ball points* have a smooth, rounded point. These are good for knitted fabrics. The needle pushes between the fibers of the fabric rather than piercing it as the sharp points do. These needles help eliminate skipped stitches *somewhat*.
3. *Wedge points* are needles with a chisel-shaped point. They are effective on vinyl and leathers. They cut a tiny slot for each stitch. This slot closes over the thread and prevents a hole from remaining. This needle will not perforate the material as a sharp point would do.

Marking Pencils:

Tailor's chalk and dressmaker's pencils with a little brush eraser on the end are available at notion counters. However, you can use any soft, water soluble pencils that can be sharpened. Get them at any hobby or art shop. They don't have the little brush on the end, like the dressmaker's pencils, but they are cheaper, last longer, and come in every color.

Make sure they are water soluble so marks can be easily and completely removed.

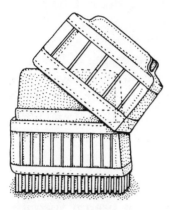

A: Tailor's chalk with a sharpening groove in the cover

B: Dressmaker's pencil with a brush eraser

Pincushion:

Get the kind that looks like a fat tomato with a strawberry attached to it. Using a pincushion is a good way to keep your pins and needles together and easy to use. A pincushion is available that has a plastic bracelet attached to it. You can wear this on your wrist while you are sewing, to keep pins handy whenever you need them.

The strawberry contains emery, a mild

Pincushion with an emery-filled strawberry

polishing agent used to keep needles and pins smooth, sharp, and shiny. Run your needles and pins through the strawberry occasionally. They will be easier to use.

Ruler:

A clear plastic one is superior for all purposes. You can see through it and measure in two directions at the same time without moving the ruler. Try to find one with black lines because they are clearly visible on all colors and patterns of fabric, even dark ones. The best one, in my opinion, is Model B85 made by C-Thru. It is 2″ wide and 18″ long.

Scissors:

Eight-inch shears are ideal for cutting all fabrics. Never use them to cut paper or they will dull quickly. Use a pair of old scissors for cutting paper. A pair of thread nippers is helpful for quickly snipping threads. A small pair of embroidery scissors with very sharp points makes trimming seams and delicate jobs easier.

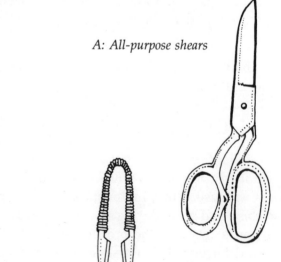

A: All-purpose shears

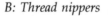

B: Thread nippers

C: Embroidery scissors

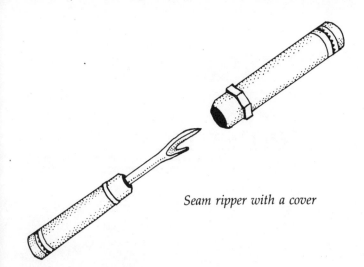

Seam ripper with a cover

Seam ripper:

This gadget can make the unpleasant job of removing stitches bearable. Choose one with a cap and a fine point. Keep it covered to prevent accidents to yourself or your project.

Sewing Machine:

One that does good straight stitching as well as zigzag stitching is best. Become familiar with your machine. Practice with it and its special attachments. The owner's manual isn't the exciting reading that makes a book a Best Seller, but it will explain the machine and show you how it can save time and produce good results that will make you proud.

Straight Pins:

Silk pins are good for general purposes. Don't leave pins in your fabric for long periods of time. They may make rust marks, discolor the fabric, or leave large, ugly holes that are difficult to remove.

Thimbles and tape measure

Tape Measure:

Choose one with metal tips that will *not* tear or stretch with use. The most durable ones are made from plastic-covered cloth or fiberglass.

Thimble:

Find one in your size that fits snugly, and learn to use it for all hand sewing. It protects your middle finger as you push the needle through the fabric.

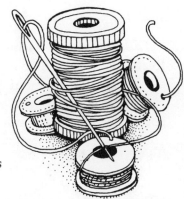

Thread and sewing machine bobbins

Thread:

Mercerized cotton in size 50 is excellent for machine or hand work and comes in all colors. Quilting thread is available in a limited number of colors. It is heavier (size 40) and has a glazed finish that makes it stiff and very durable. Heavy duty thread is good for projects that will get lots of roughing up, like the duffle bag in Project 4.

Tracing Paper and Tracing Wheel:

You can transfer designs quickly and easily from pattern to fabric this way. They often come packaged together with instructions in the sewing notions department. See Part One, Chapter Four: Adapting, Enlarging, and Transferring Your Designs, for further explanation of using a tracing wheel.

The tracing wheel

CHAPTER TWO

Some Terms to Remember

Appliqué:

The method of attaching one piece of fabric to another by stitching is called appliqué. You apply smaller cut-out pieces to a larger background piece. The pieces are cut with templates and interpret a design or picture.

Backing Fabric

(Or Quilt Backing): The layer that is on the underside of a quilted piece. It is usually a solid color that contrasts or blends with the quilt top. It is on the bottom during stitching. Many quilts are reversible; the fabric and stitching on the backing fabric should be as good as that on the top fabric.

Bias:

Any direction that is not parallel to the lengthwise or crosswise grain is a bias. It will stretch and drape softly. A true bias runs at a 45° angle to either the lengthwise or crosswise grain. It has maximum "give" and will hang or drape better than a bias cut at any other angle.

Broadcloth:

A closely-woven, lightweight but durable fabric. It comes in many solid colors, textures, and fibers. Cotton or cotton blend broadcloth is best for most of the projects in this book because it is easy to handle. It does not fray readily, and it holds its shape well.

Corded Quilting:

Close parallel lines of stitching (about ¼" apart) that are later filled with cord or yarn. This is a purely decorative technique. The top fabric is a plain, smooth-woven material. Muslin makes a perfect backing fabric. A strictly linear design is best for this method.

Echo Quilting:

Making rows of quilting stitches that surround a motif and imitate its shape is called echo quilting. The distances between the rows need not be equal. Imagine the rings that are formed by dropping a stone in a puddle.

Fabric Fuser:

Two layers of fabric can be joined together without stitching by using a fabric fuser. This is a weblike synthetic material that is sold by the yard or in packages. It can be cut like fabric into any shape needed. It melts when it is placed between two layers of fabric and heated with an iron.

It has many uses, but it is especially good for holding intricate appliqué pieces in place for stitching. Experiment with the fuser and scrap fabric to test the technique and your iron temperature.

Avoid any contact with the metal surface of your iron and the right sides of your project. It is very difficult to remove any unwanted fuser without leaving a gummy residue. Don't leave any stray scraps on the ironing board that could melt accidentally and ruin something. Follow the instructions that come with the fuser very carefully.

Filler:

In quilting, whatever material is sandwiched between the top and backing fabrics is referred to as filler. It could be batting, fleece, or a piece cut from an old blanket. Loose filler such as polyester fluff is used for pillows. If you would rather not buy loose filler, use discarded nylon stockings. Launder them, and cut them up into small pieces. Yarn and tiny fabric clippings are also a good substitute.

Fleece:

A very thin, pressed type of batting is called fleece. It is ⅛″ to ¼″ thick and is used for quilting when a very raised, puffed effect is *not* desired. Soft, white, preshrunk flannel fabric can be used as a good substitute.

Grain:

The direction of the weave of a piece of fabric is called grain. The lengthwise grain runs parallel to the selvages. The crosswise grain runs across the fabric between the selvages. It is perpendicular to the lengthwise grain and is often the weaker grain.

Grid:

The intersecting lines on graph paper form a grid. They intersect at even intervals. You may need to draw your own grid to enlarge a small design from graph paper. (see Adapting, Enlarging, and Transferring Your Designs, p. 25.)

Hem:

There are many kinds of hems. They can be sewn by machine or by hand. Fabric edges are doubled back to the wrong side and stitched in place to prevent unraveling and to give a finished appearance to the raw edges.

Interfacing:

Specially treated, woven and non-woven fabrics that are used to stiffen and support other fabrics are known as interfacing. They come in a variety of weights and fibers. Experiment with several different types until you find the interfacing that you like working with best. A good selection of fusible interfacings is available. They come in woven and non-woven types. Instructions for attaching the interfacing should come with it. Check to be sure you have them. They all work in the same basic way. One side has a heat sensitive surface that melts when you iron on the other side. This melting bonds the interfacing to the fabric. Position it very carefully; it can't always be removed successfully. Don't ever place your iron down on the "coated" side of a fusible interfacing.

Miter:

The joint of two straight pieces at a 45° angle is called a miter. Mitering eliminates bulkiness when ribbon or fabric makes a corner. The resulting seam is a 45° angle and resembles the corner of a picture frame. (See Easy Sewing Fundamentals to Master, p. 36.)

Muslin:

Plain-woven cotton fabric is called muslin. It comes bleached (white) or unbleached (off-white) in different weights and grades of fineness. Make sure that it is preshrunk before using it.

Non-woven:

Fabrics that are not composed of threads intersecting at right angles are non-woven. The most common example of this is felt. Quilt batting and fleece are also non-woven. To check your fabric, hold it up to a light. Look through it to find a weave. The surface of some woven fabrics appears to be non-woven. This fuzzy outer surface is brushed up during manufacturing, and it disguises the weave.

Outline Quilting:

Quilting stitches that go around the perimeter of a design or motif and separate it from the background are called outline quilting. It is usually one row of stitching and is often used to emboss or accentuate printed designs.

Patchwork:

To make patchwork, you seam many small pieces of fabric together in a planned design. The finished piece is one layer of fabric throughout, with the exception of the seam allowances.

Quilt

(As a verb): The process of sewing two or more layers of fabric together is called quilting. Usually a soft filler is placed between the top and the backing layers.

Quilt

(As a noun): A quilt is a bedspread or bed-size cover that is made up using the quilting technique. The three layers (top, filler, and backing) are held together by hand or machine stitches that are done in a planned quilting design or diagram.

Quilt Top

(Or Top Fabric): The piece of fabric that is used as the upper layer in quilting is called the quilt top. It can be plain or decorative. Quilt tops are frequently made from printed fabric, patchwork, embroidery, and appliqué. This layer is on the top during quilting.

Reverse Appliqué:

This type of appliqué layers two to eight pieces of different colored broadcloth that are all the same size. Designs are made by cutting through one layer at a time to expose each different color underneath.

Seam Allowance:

The narrow border of fabric that is included in a pattern beyond the finished seamline is the seam allowance. It can vary between ¼" and one inch depending on the fabric and the intricacy of the work. Intricate patchwork requires a ¼" seam allowance. All the projects in this book use a standard ½" seam allowance.

Selvage:

The two tightly woven edges that run lengthwise along the outer edges of fabric yard goods are called selvages. The selvage does not ravel. Trim off the selvage. Don't use it in a project; it will shrink more than the fabric itself. This uneven shrinking of the selvage will draw up the seams of a project and cause puckering.

Shadow Appliqué:

Layering two or more translucent fabrics such as chiffon or organdy to achieve blending and change of color is shadow or translucent appliqué. For example, red placed over yellow would make a third color, orange.

Stuffed Quilting

(Sometimes called Trapunto): Stitching pockets in two layers of fabric and stuffing them through a slash made in the wrong side is known as stuffed quilting. Motifs for this method should be solid enclosed shapes. An interesting, soft look is achieved by using a translucent top fabric and colored yarn as stuffing.

Top Stitching:

Machine or hand stitching that is done after seams are sewn is called top-stitching. It can be purely decorative or used to add strength and durability to seams. It also flattens seams and gives them a very professional finish.

CHAPTER THREE

A Few Preparations Before Sewing

COLORFAST TESTING

Always test the fabrics that you are using, despite what you have been told at the fabric shop. Imported fabrics are especially questionable. You can tell if the dyes are "set" (permanent) on a piece of fabric by placing a swatch of the fabric in a bowl of very hot water. If there is a lot of dye released into the water after a few minutes, you can be certain that the dyes will run and spoil your finished project. You can do several things to correct very runny dyes:

1. Wash the fabric in hot soapy water several times until the rinse water runs clear. This will sometimes remove a great amount of the color. It also will soften the fabric nicely, making it more subtle in appearance and easier to handle.

2. If the fabric runs very badly, you need to take another step. Boil the fabric in a large pot with ½ cup of white vinegar for about an hour. Follow this by washing. Include an old white cotton handkerchief in the wash with the fabric. If the handkerchief stays white, the dye has been set. This is a long, messy way to start out a project, so be sure that the fabric is worth your trouble. Test the vinegar solution on a swatch of the fabric before beginning to see how effective it will be.

3. Bleaching will remove the dye from your fabric. The stronger the bleach and water solution, the more color you will lose. It is also

good for removing heavy fabric finishes such as waterproofing, glazing, permanent press, etcetera. Test the strength of your solution of water and bleach carefully. A too-strong solution will deteriorate the fabric so that it falls apart or wears out very quickly. For example, over-bleached jeans will tear easily and develop worn spots very fast.

ESTIMATING YARDAGE

When you are designing a project yourself, or you are not sure how much fabric is required for a project, you will need to estimate the yardage yourself. To do this, first make the patterns or templates of the pieces that you will be cutting out. Make a small chart as follows:

Color of Fabric	Number of pieces to cut out	Approximate size of one piece	Yardage required
Red	12	6" x 8"	½ yard
Blue	24	10" x 12"	2 yards

To get the approximate size of each pattern piece, measure the size of the patterns. Be sure to include a seam allowance. Don't skimp; give yourself room to turn the pattern in a different direction if needed. If you are using stripes, you may want to lay out each piece in a specific direction. Also some fabric has designs printed on it, such as flowers or animals, that are spaced far apart. Center the pattern pieces over these parts of the fabric. If you know what fabric you are using, you will know how closely the pattern pieces can be placed.

After you have determined the approximate size of each piece, divide the width of the pattern (in inches) into the width of your fabric (probably 44" to 45" wide). This tells you how many pieces can be cut in one row across the fabric. Next, divide the height of the pattern (in inches) into 36" (one yard of fabric). This figure will tell you how many rows you can get in one yard of fabric. For example, I need twelve red pieces that measure approximately 6" x 8". My fabric is 45" wide. Therefore, I can get about seven pieces in one row. The rows can be repeated about four times on a yard of fabric. That's 28 pieces in one yard of 45" wide fabric. To cut out only twelve pieces, I will need ½ yard. Fill in this information on the chart you have made.

When you are buying fabric, be sure to get enough because there is no guarantee that the store will have the same thing later if you run out. Any leftover scraps can be used up in another project. Check the fabric for flaws, faded areas or misprinting before you buy it and before you cut.

PRESHRINKING

It is a good idea to preshrink all your fabrics before using them, especially if you are not sure if a fabric will shrink no more than one percent. If you are combining two different types of fabrics in one project, one of them may shrink more than the other one so be sure to preshrink everything first. A good steaming with your iron and a damp pressing cloth may be sufficient, especially for wools. Wash washable fabrics in warm to hot soapy water. This will also remove any stiffeners and fabric finishes that may affect your stitching and cause puckering. Another advantage of preshrinking is that any extra dye that remains in the fabric will be removed.

CHAPTER FOUR

Adapting, Enlarging and Transferring Your Designs

ADAPTING DESIGNS

It is not difficult to turn your own ideas into designs for decorative sewing. There is no mystery to creating your own designs or adapting an idea from a photograph or even an object. You don't have to conduct an intensive search for designs. Don't waste time waiting for a creative inspiration either. There are unlimited ideas right in your own environment. Take a careful look around you. Some of the best ideas are found in objects or things you see every day and take for granted.

Photographs and illustrations in books and magazines can provide some good designs. Look through the magazines that you like. Maybe you won't find any designs you want to use, but it gets your imagination working.

Instructions for a needlework kit or project such as needlepoint or embroidery may provide a design and perhaps a pattern. You also can buy heat transfer designs that you just iron on the fabric if you want to take the easy way out. Children's coloring books are surprisingly good design sources.

After you have decided on your design subject, you need to make a paper pattern to use for working. There are a few ways to do this; choose the method that is the simplest for your specific project.

If you like to sketch, draw your own pattern. This is the best way to make designs from small objects or very simple geometric shapes. You may even be able to trace around a portion of the object if it is flat, such as a trivet or cookie cutter. Make use of rulers,

compasses, and plastic templates as much as possible. Visit your hobby shop or art supply store. Ask to see the supplies for commercial artists. Plastic templates, French curves in all sizes, special compasses, pencils, rulers, etcetera, are the everyday tools of commercial artists. You will discover some things that will help you draw things in a much easier way.

If you are planning a design that is symmetrical, you can save yourself lots of time and trouble by using a technique that I call the *burnishing transfer technique,* which is described below. This technique works for any design that can be divided into two or four identical parts.

Fold a piece of plain paper into quarters. Draw one quarter of the design on one of the folded quarters of the paper. Go over the lines of the design with a very soft pencil. Fold the paper in half lengthwise with the design on the inside. Put the paper on a hard, flat surface. Rub or burnish the folded paper from the outside with the edge of a spoon. Use pressure. Make sure to rub over all the lines of the design. Open the paper. The design has now been burnished onto the other quarter of the paper.

Go over the lines of *both* quarters of the design with the soft pencil. Fold the paper in half crosswise. Burnish the outside of the paper over the design as before. The first two quarters of the design are now transferred to the second half of the paper simultaneously.

If the lines of the design are faint or fuzzy, go over them to clarify them.

This method works for designs that are the same on two or four sides. One side must be the mirror-image of the other. You may only need to fold and burnish once for some designs. Any drawing can be burnished off in this way to another piece of paper. Remember that the burnished version of the design will be in the opposite direction as if you saw it in a mirror.

Designs that repeat the same motif over and over again require only one pattern that can be moved around and used as many times as desired.

Make your sketch in pencil so that you can correct and change it as often as you like. When you are satisfied with the design, go over the final lines with a felt tip marker. Neatness doesn't count. This is only a pattern, not a piece of art.

If you enjoy photography or know someone who does, use this as a way to capture a design. This works especially well if you are using a large subject, such as a landscape or architectural detail. To avoid expensive printing and enlarging, take slide photographs. You can project the slide onto a piece of paper taped to the wall. Move the projector forward or backward until the design is the size that you want. Draw around the design, being careful not to move the projector until you have finished. Turn the room lights on every so often to check your progress.

An opaque projector will enlarge a design from a book or magazine. Tape a piece of paper to the wall and proceed to draw in the same way as described in the method using a slide projector.

Flat pictures or drawings can be traced directly from the original using one of the methods below under Transferring Designs. If the design is not the correct size, it can be reduced or enlarged by using the grid method found below under Enlarging Designs or by use of an opaque projector.

Even if you plan to copy a design, don't hesitate to change it if there are certain parts or colors that you don't like. Feel free to eliminate completely sections of the design. If you aren't happy with a particular flower or leaf, change it or forget it altogether.

Try to simplify a very complex design. Photographs especially will change dramatically when you make line drawings from them. They will resemble cartoons or caricatures. Simplify as much as necessary. If you know that you will be working with very thick fabric, tiny, delicate pieces will be difficult to handle. Choose a design that will work well with the sewing technique that you will be using.

Remember that no matter how you adapt your design, it is your own version of the original item. It is not an exact duplicate, and you don't want it to be. No matter how hard you try, you will not be able to do certain things with fabrics. Work with fabrics that you will be using; experiment and find out what works best.

You can't make your sewing pictures look like a photograph of the real thing so don't even try. Adapting your own designs only seems difficult. The more designs you do, the easier it becomes to interpret objects. Make your own personal statement about things, trust yourself . . . and you can, too, draw a straight line!

ENLARGING DESIGNS

A photostat service will enlarge or reduce any type of photo or design photographically. This is usually expensive, but it is good if you are in a hurry, or if you want to see your design in several different sizes before you decide on what size you want to use.

You can easily enlarge your own designs or something from a book by using the grid technique. You may draw your own grid, or you can buy special graph paper that has ½" or 1" squares printed on it at an art supply store. You must begin with a design that is drawn on a grid or a piece of graph paper. You

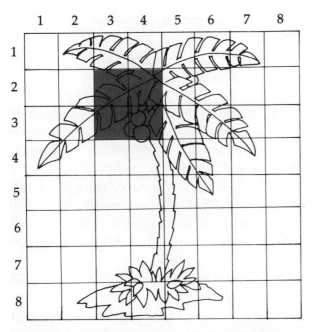

A square grid drawn over a design or photograph

Four squares enlarged exactly from the shaded area of the original design

The shaded square enlarged

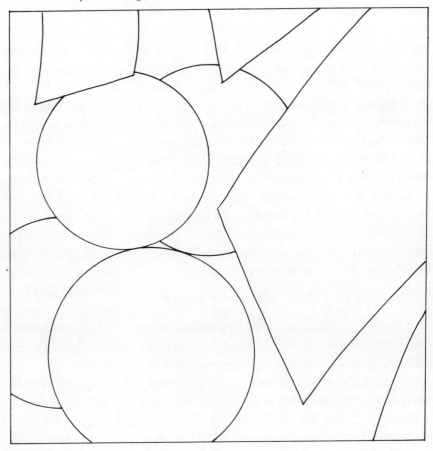

can copy a design from a magazine photo or anything else by drawing a grid of squares on top of it. I keep a piece of tracing paper or clear acetate handy with a ¼" grid drawn on it so that I can place it on top of anything that I want to copy. Some stores sell tracing paper with a grid printed on it.

Number the rows of squares on your grid from the upper left corner out vertically and horizontally. Make a second, larger grid. If you want the design twice as large, use squares that are twice as large as the ones of the grid on the original design. You can make the design any size you wish by just varying the size of the squares on the larger grid. The large grid should have the same number of squares as the original one. The enlargement that you make will be perfect in scale to the original.

For example: The palm tree is covered by a ¼" grid that has eight squares horizontally and vertically, or sixty-four ¼" squares. If I want my finished design to be 8" square, I would draw a larger grid of sixty-four 1" squares. For enlarging it to 12" x 12", the grid would contain sixty-four 1½" squares. For enlarging it to 16" x 16", the grid would contain sixty-four 2" squares, and so on.

Copy one square at a time from your small grid to the large grid. You can estimate or use a ruler to help you check distances. For example: The coconuts are in the lower left corner of square number three in column four. The lowest coconut on the left extends outside the square. It curves out of the square at the center of the gridline and curves back in just slightly above the bottom of the gridline.

REDUCING DESIGNS

A large design can also be reduced by using the grid technique. Follow the instructions that are given for enlarging designs with the following exceptions. Since you are beginning with a large design, you will start by drawing a large grid over it. You can copy the large squares into the small squares one at a time.

This is simply the reverse of the technique of Enlarging Designs.

TRANSFERRING DESIGNS

Throughout this book you will need to know how to transfer a design from paper to fabric. This can be done equally well by any of the following methods.

If your design is square, find the fabric center by folding it into fourths. Mark this point with a pin and center the paper pattern over it. Working flat, pin the design to the right side of the fabric in its proper position. Select a piece of dressmaker's carbon paper in a color that will show up well on the fabric. Make a test on a scrap of your fabric to be sure the carbon marks can be washed out easily. Slip the carbon paper between the design and the right side of the fabric with the carbon side against the fabric. You may need to do one section of the design at a time if the carbon is not large enough to fit under the entire design at once.

Using the tracing wheel, follow the lines of the design in the area where the carbon paper is located. Hold the pattern down flat as you work. You will perforate the pattern, and the carbon will transfer the lines to the fabric.

Move the carbon paper as often as necessary. When the entire design is perforated, you will have transferred it completely. This method is good for most designs; however, you damage your pattern, and it will fall apart after repeated uses. The dotted lines made by the tracing wheel are not very clear on some fabrics, especially wools and printed fabrics. Make a test piece to check visibility of the carbon.

The second method is done by cutting out a cardboard copy of your design. This serves as a template or a pattern that you can draw around. After centering the pattern on the right side of the fabric, hold it in place with the fingers of one hand and draw around the edges with the other hand. Use a soft pencil or chalk that can be removed later. This method is especially good because you can repeat a design many times, and you don't ruin the template.

If you use the third method, you need not make a template and the design remains intact. You need to find a window at a fairly low height that you can use to draw over. Go over the lines of your original design so that they are as dark as possible.

Tape the design to the window. Place your fabric, right side toward you, over the sketch so that the design is in the desired position. Tape the fabric in place. Using a soft pencil or chalk, lightly trace the lines of the design onto the right side of the fabric.

If you have a table with a glass or plexiglass top, you can use it in the same way by placing a light on the floor beneath the table. This is a makeshift version of a professional light table.

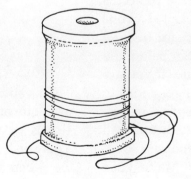

CHAPTER FIVE

Stitches You Will Need to Know

Backstitch:

If you are not using a sewing machine to make your projects, the backstitch is the strongest of the hand stitches. Following the seamline, take one stitch back that is about 1/16″ to ¼″ long. Push the needle out about 1/16″ to ¼″ forward along the seamline. Try to keep your stitches spaced evenly. Always in-

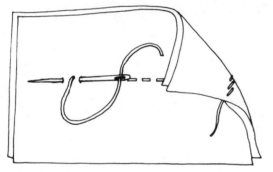

Backstitch

sert your needle next to the end of the last stitch and come out one stitch ahead. The back of your work should have long overlapping stitches.

Basting Stitch:

Basting stitches are not permanent, and they are generally removed when a project is completed. Basting is sometimes called an un-even running stitch. It is perfect for holding seams and layers of fabric together before the final stitching is done by machine. If you are matching stripes or plaids, it is a good idea to baste pieces together first to assure a perfect match. Take one ¼″ long stitch through all layers of the fabric; skip across about ½″ or 1″ and take a second ¼″ stitch. Make your

stitches smaller if the fabric is slippery or difficult to manage.

Most stores sell special basting thread. It is weaker and not as fine quality as regular thread. Use it only for basting because it may break easily. Occasionally basting thread has slubs and imperfections on it. It will not go through a sewing machine well. The slubs

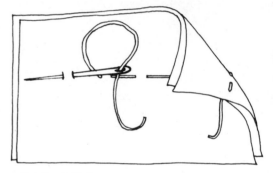

Basting stitch

cause jamming at the eye of the needle and possibly machine tension problems. It is generally found in white only on spools that hold 1,200 to 2,000 yards of thread. It is perfect for temporary hand work and is very inexpensive. You will probably use it often, but one large spool will last a long time.

Blanket Stitch:

This stitch is used to overcast an edge or to appliqué one fabric to another. Take one stitch that is ⅛″ to ¼″ from the edge of the fabric. This stitch will emerge at the edge of the fabric. Keep the loop of the thread under the

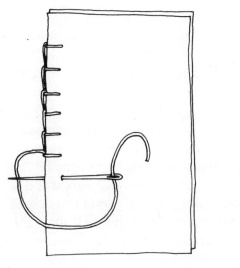

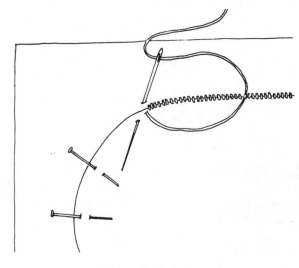

Blanket stitch   *Outline stitch*   *Overhand stitch*

needle as it emerges from the underside of the edge. Pull the stitch so that it is snug. Take a second stitch in the same manner. The thread will be carried along the edge of the fabric. The spaces between the stitches, as well as the depth of the stitches can be varied according to the result desired.

Outline Stitch:

This is an embroidery stitch that is used to cover a raw edge or delineate a design. It is done in a contrasting color with yarn or embroidery floss. It has a tiny, twisted, rope-like appearance. Working diagonally, make close, parallel stitches that are all the same length. It is done like the backstitch and is sometimes called the stem stitch.

Overhand Stitch:

This stitch is used to appliqué one piece to another. It is a good, strong stitch that is fast and easy to do. The stitches are perpendicular to the edge of the fabric. Insert the needle into the fabric right across from the last stitch. The needle goes through the fabric diagonally to the next stitch. Make all the stitches the same size and evenly spaced.

Overcast Stitch:

Any stitch that wraps or covers the raw edge of the fabric is an overcasting stitch. It is usually done on a single layer of fabric. To overcast by hand, work a stitch similar to the whipstitch (described below) around the raw edge of the fabric. Use the machine zigzag or one of the special machine embroidery stitches for overcasting. Check your manual for special features on your machine for overcasting. The more the fabric frays, the closer the stitches should be.

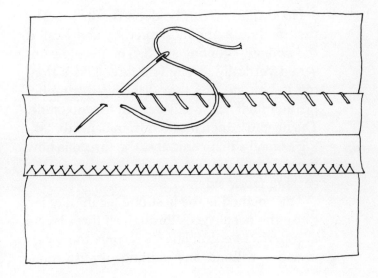

Overcast stitch

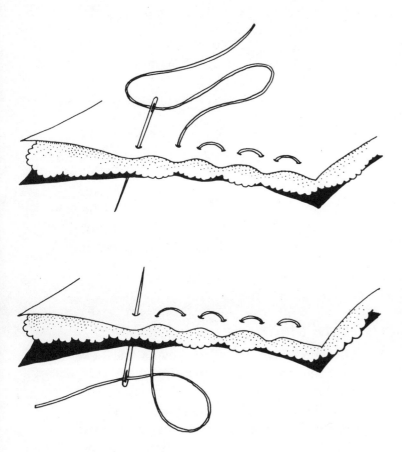

Quilting stitch: Two-step method

This is, however, just like the best way of doing almost anything: the more difficult way.

If the quilted piece is being held with an embroidery hoop or frame, one hand remains underneath to return the needle to the top. The other hand (your writing hand) pushes the needle from the top down to the underneath hand. Your stitches can be as small or large as you like . . . generally the smaller the better. Find a stitch size that looks good and is easy for you to do. This technique works well for very thick layers of quilting. It does the difficult job of holding many thicknesses together so that they are very flat and even.

If your quilted piece is rather thin, or you haven't mastered the two-step stitch, use the second method. Make sure all three layers are well-basted together.

Working entirely from the top, insert your needle through all three layers. Take a small stitch on the backing fabric and return the point of the needle to the top in one step. With practice, you can load several identical stitches on your needle at once.

With this one-step method, the needle penetrates the three layers at an angle. This causes the layers to shift somewhat. Make lots of rows of basting that are very close together to eliminate this problem.

This one-step technique is easier to learn to do. It also is faster than the two-step method.

Quilting Stitch:

Hand quilting can be done two ways. The first method is the most precise, and I call it the two-step quilting stitch. The needle is inserted vertically through all three layers from top to bottom. The thread is pulled from beneath until it lies snugly against the top fabric. The needle is then inserted from beneath, taking a small stitch vertically. The thread is now pulled from the top until it is snug on the backing fabric side.

This method is the best one technically because the needle goes through all three layers in a perfect vertical line. It secures the layers together without any shifting or distortion.

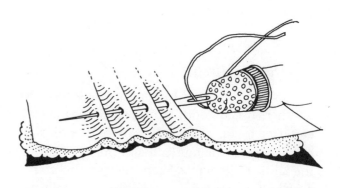

Quilting stitch: One-step method

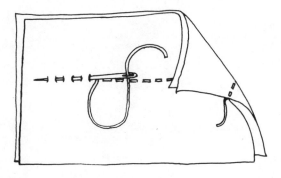

Running stitch

Running Stitch:

This is a very basic and versatile stitch. It is good for seams and all general sewing. Working in a straight line, take two to four stitches forward, going through all layers of the fabric. Try to make your stitches between 1/16" and ¼" long. The smaller the stitches, the more durable they will be. A large, even or uneven, running stitch is perfect for basting.

Satin Stitch:

Close parallel rows of straight embroidery stitches that make a smooth surface are called the satin stitch. The length of each stitch is determined by the amount of space that needs to be filled. The stitches begin and end along the edge of the shape that needs to be covered. They are done with yarn or embroidery floss.

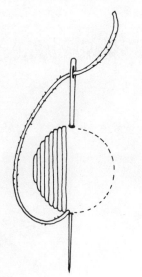

Satin stitch

Slipstitch:

Use this stitch to hand finish one edge to another, such as a hem. Two creased edges of fabric can be joined almost invisibly using this stitch. It can be done evenly or unevenly as follows:

Insert your needle into the creased edge of the fabric. Push the needle along inside the crease for the length of one stitch. At the point where the needle emerges from the crease, take a stitch in the other side just beneath the crease. This stitch should be placed so it is not visible when the two layers are flat. Both stitches should be the same length. Pull the thread through both stitches at one time. Make a series of stitches in this manner. When completed, the stitches will not show on the working side.

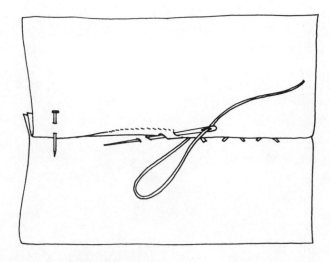

Slipstitch

If you are doing a hem or an edge and you want the stitches on the underside to be invisible as well, use the uneven slipstitch. Take a stitch in the creased edge as with the even slipstitch. The second stitch should pick up only one or two threads of the fabric underneath. Immediately return the needle into the creased edge. The stitches in the creased edge should all be the same length.

Whipstitch:

This stitch is used for general hand sewing. It joins two fabric edges together. An equal amount of fabric is caught on both sides of the edges. The needle is inserted into the fabric perpendicular to the edge. The resulting stitches are diagonal. A very loose whipstitch is used to piece quilt batting when necessary.

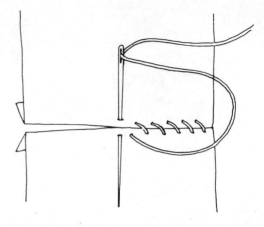

Whipstitch

CHAPTER SIX

Preparing the Fabric For Cutting

STRAIGHTENING THE FABRIC

Throughout this book, you will need to make a straight edge on your fabric in order to cut out a square. There are several methods that are appropriate.

For tightly woven, firm fabrics, tearing along the crossgrain is the quickest and best method.

For more loosely woven fabrics that may stretch out of shape if they are torn, use the following method: Clip the selvage and free one crossgrain thread. Pull this thread carefully across the crossgrain. Slide the fabric as you pull, creating a slightly gathered effect. Repeat this across the entire piece and cut along this thread.

If your fabric has a thick or obvious weave, such as a plaid, you can easily cut along one cross-thread. Make sure the plaid is woven rather than printed by looking at the wrong side. Printed plaids are often crooked.

SQUARING OFF THE FABRIC

Pin the straightened edge or selvage of your fabric to an ironing board, or lay it flat on a table. Place your L square so that one side is aligned with the straightened edge at the top. The other side of the L square should line up with the selvage or lengthwise grain. If it does not match, stretch the fabric on the bias. To do this, grasp one upper corner in one hand and

the diagonally opposite corner in the other hand. Pull firmly several times, and then use the L square to check your results. When the two sides of the L square line up with the lengthwise and crosswise grain lines, you are ready to measure and cut out a perfect square.

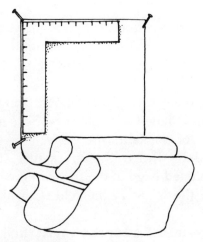

Squaring off the fabric

PRESSING

Press all your fabrics before you use them. This is the perfect way to check for any flaws, dirt spots, fading, etcetera. It is a good idea to test the temperature of your iron on a corner or a scrap piece before placing it in the center of the fabric.

CHAPTER SEVEN

Easy Sewing Fundamentals to Master

BIAS STRIPS

True bias strips are cut from fabric yardage for use as ruffles, binding, or piping. You can buy bias tape and piping in a limited number of solid colors and a few prints. If you want to use a special fabric or need to match an unusual color, you will want to cut your own bias strips.

Make sure you have at least one yard of the fabric that you want to use. Straighten the cut edge of the fabric as described in the previous chapter.

Fold the yardage diagonally, bringing the raw straightened edge of the fabric to meet the selvage of the fabric. A perfect 45° angle is formed by the fold that results. Pin the straightened edge of the fabric to the selvage. Crease the fabric at the fold. Cut along the crease.

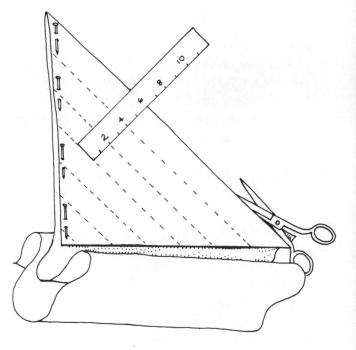

Folding and cutting a true bias strip

Draw lines 2″ away from and parallel to the foldline that you have cut. Pin the two layers of fabric together to prevent slipping when you cut out the 2″ strips. Measure the length of the bias strips, and cut out as many as you will need to complete your project.

Seam these bias strips together by making a diagonal seam as follows: Place the right sides of the fabric together and match the short edges. The strips should form a right angle as they are put together because of the 45° angled edge at the short end of each strip. Pin and stitch a seam ½″ away from the short edges. The seam should follow the grain of the fabric. Press the seam open.

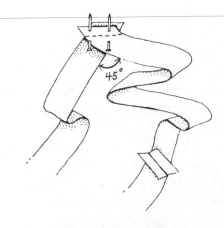

Seaming bias strips together

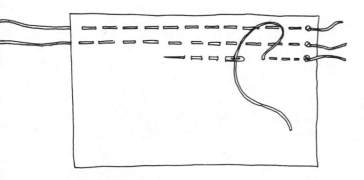

Making parallel rows of stitching for gathering

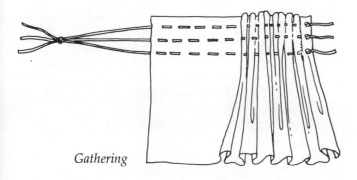

Gathering

GATHERING

Gathering is a basic method that you need to know for several of the projects in this book. It can be done by any of these three methods.

By machine

Use the largest stitch on your machine, and make one row of stitching ¼" away from the cut edge on the right side of your fabric. Leave the thread ends about 3" long. Make a second row of stitching in the same way that is about ¼" away from the first row. Working from one edge, knot the two *bobbin* threads together and pull them gently. Ease the gathers to the center of the piece and adjust them evenly to one half of the finished length. Repeat this from the opposite end. Be careful not to pull the thread too vigorously as it will snap, and you will have to begin again. If you are gathering heavy or thick fabric, you should use a heavy duty thread in the bobbin of your machine.

By hand

Any fabric can be gathered nicely by using two or three rows of short, even running stitches parallel to the cut edge of the fabric. Knot the two or three ends together and pull them simultaneously as described in the machine method.

Zigzag stitching over cord or string

A very fast technique of gathering uses the machine zigzag stitch. Set your machine so that the stitches it makes are as wide as possible and make about eight zigzags per inch. Cut a piece of cord or light-weight string that measures the same length as the *finished* gathers you need. Knot both ends. Working on the wrong side, begin ½" from the raw edge. Place the knot in the cord behind the presser foot of your machine. Work about four or five stitches by hand turning the wheel. Continue the zigzag stitch over the cording, being very careful not to catch the cording with the needle. Stop the machine; and gently pull the cording. The fabric will gather up behind the presser foot. Work across the entire piece in this manner until the knot in the other end of the cord is at the other end of the gathered piece.

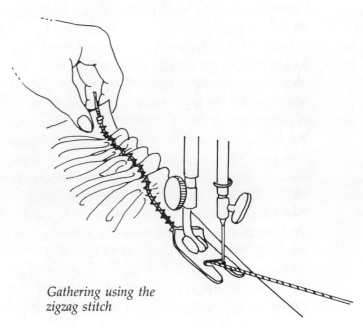

Gathering using the zigzag stitch

GRADING SEAMS

To eliminate bulk and thickness when seams are pressed together in one direction, you will want to grade the edges. This is done by trimming each layer of the seam allowances to a different width. Trim off about ⅛" of each layer working toward the *inside* of the project. A seam that contains piping will have four layers to trim.

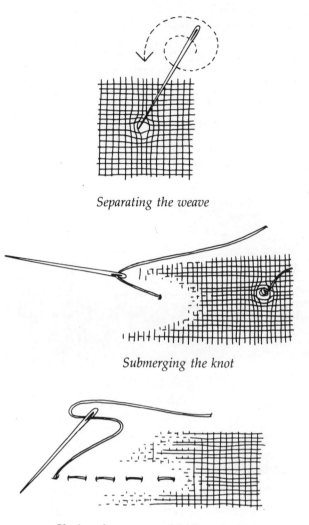

Separating the weave

Submerging the knot

Closing the weave and hiding the knot

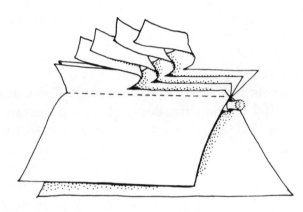

Grading a seam that has piping

HIDING A QUILTING KNOT

When you are hand sewing, you'll get a much nicer finish if the thread knots are not visible. To hide a knot easily during quilting, push the point of your needle into the fabric about ½" away from where your stitching is to begin. Move the needle in a circular motion, thereby separating the weave of the fabric slightly. Insert the needle into this opening and emerge at the point where you wish to begin sewing. Pull the thread gently through the top fabric and filler until the knot pops into the opening that you made with the point of the needle. The knot will submerge itself in the filler and not be visible from either side. Rub your finger gently over the opening you made in the weave, and the hole will disappear.

To end a length of thread, take a tiny back stitch or two. Hide the end of the thread by inserting the needle into the last back stitch and emerging about ½" away. Snip the thread off close to the surface, and the end will disappear into the filler.

KNOTTING THE ENDS OF YOUR THREADS

Seams and all types of hand sewing should be knotted in some way to prevent unraveling.

For hand basting it is best to make a tiny back stitch rather than a knot. This permits the stitches to be removed quickly and easily.

Most hand sewing is started with a knot in the end of the thread. Snip the end of the thread that comes from the spool at an angle for easy threading. Don't ever break it or use your teeth to tear the thread. Thread the needle with this end, and pull about 12" to 18" of thread through the eye of the needle from the spool. Knot this same end of the thread as follows: Wrap the end of the thread around your index finger. Hold it in place and gently roll the thread between your forefinger and thumb. Slip this twisted loop off of your finger and pull it with your fingernail and thumbnail until a small knot is formed. Practice this a bit if you have never done it before. You will quickly be able to make tiny, tight, perfectly round little knots. Snip the thread coming from the spool about 6" from the needle. Thread inserted into a needle in this direction will knot and tangle less because the twist of the thread will be smoothed down as it is pulled through the fabric.

To finish off your hand sewing, first, pull the needle to the wrong side of your work and take a tiny stitch (about 1/16" long) in the fabric. As your needle emerges from this stitch, wrap the thread that is closest to the needle around the point of the needle twice. Hold this wrapped spot with your thumb and pull the needle out of the fabric and through the wrapping. Pull this knot slowly and snugly against the fabric. Submerge the end of the thread by taking a stitch between the layers of fabric that begins at the knot. Clip the thread off where it emerges from the fabric.

If you are using a sewing machine, there are two ways to secure the end of the threads. The first is to make three or four stitches in reverse at the beginning and end of seams or rows of stitching. This is called backtracking or security stitching. If your machine does not have a reverse stitch, you can make reverse stitches by beginning about ½" inside the raw edge. Sew toward the raw edge, stop at the edge, pivot your work around and stitch back over the ½" of reverse stitching. Complete the seam. Pivot the work around and stitch back over the end of the seam for about ½".

The second is used when stitching ends in the center of a piece of work, such as in machine quilting. It is important in this case to secure the ends of stitching invisibly. Stop stitching wherever you like. Remove your work from the machine. Cut the threads about 6" or 8" from the stitching. Turn your piece over and pull the bobbin thread gently. A loop will appear. Insert a pin into this loop and pull the upper thread through to the back of the work. Tie the bobbin thread and the upper thread together with a square knot. Insert both ends into a needle. Hide the thread ends by inserting the needle back into the fabric. Emerge about 1" away. Remove the needle and snip the thread ends close to the fabric. The knot and thread ends will be almost undetectable.

MITERING RIBBON, ETCETERA

Two straight pieces of ribbon or fabric can be joined at a 45° angle to form a corner like that of a picture frame. The seam that is formed is a diagonal seam between the two pieces. This type of finishing is decorative, and it eliminates bulkiness at corners.

Fold a piece of ribbon or a band of fabric in half with the right sides together. Match the sides and pin them together. Fold down the folded end so that it meets one of the side edges. Crease along the 45° angle fold that is formed. Open this fold out and pin the diagonal creases together. Stitch on the creaseline. Trim off the excess corner about ¼" from the seamline. Open the seam and press open. Tuck under the seam allowances at the outer corner, and press them so that they don't show.

MITERING HEMS

Hemmed edges can also be mitered at a corner. This makes an even, neat, flat corner. This is a good way to hem dinner napkins or any square piece of fabric. You can make these hems very narrow or very wide. It looks very professional and is really easy. Try it!

Press under ¼" toward the wrong side on all the edges that you want to hem. Next, press under the hem. It can be any width hem you like. Generally, hems range between ¼"

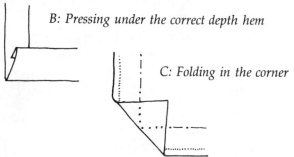

A: Pressing under ¼" on all sides

B: Pressing under the correct depth hem

C: Folding in the corner

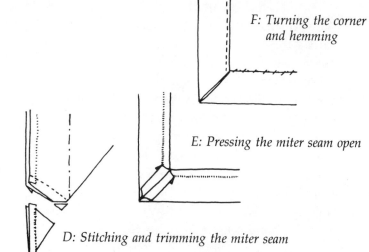

F: Turning the corner and hemming

E: Pressing the miter seam open

D: Stitching and trimming the miter seam

and 3", depending on the weight of the fabric and what looks best.

Open out the corners of the hem. Leave the ¼" pressed edge in place. Fold down the corner at the intersection of the hem creases. Press the diagonal fold.

Open the corner again. Fold the fabric in half, with the right sides together, through the creased corner point. Match the edges and the diagonal crease lines. Stitch across the corner on the diagonal crease lines. Trim off the corner ¼" from your stitching. Trim the point. Press this seam open. Turn the corner right side out. Carefully push out the point with the tip of your scissors. Now finish the hem by hand or machine.

NOTCHING AND CLIPPING

When you are working with curved seams or edges, it is necessary to notch or clip the seam allowances so that the curve will be smooth and the fabric will lie flat.

An outward curved or convex seam, such as the outside edge of a circle, will have a bulky seam allowance when it is turned to the inside. Notching the seam allowance eliminates this problem. Clip tiny V-shaped wedges from the seam allowance as often as necessary to make it lie flat. The points of the wedges should be at least ⅛" away from the stitching.

An inward or concave seam, such as the hole in a doughnut, must be clipped before it can be turned at all. Carefully clip the seam allowances as often as needed to permit turning. The clips should be at least ⅛" away from the stitching.

OVERCASTING

Any stitch that wraps or covers a raw edge with thread can be considered overcasting. The purpose of this stitching is to finish the raw seam edges and prevent them from unraveling when they are worn and washed. Overcasting seams lengthens the life of a garment and makes it neatly finished inside. It doesn't take much additional time at all so it is well worth the effect.

The zigzag stitch is the most commonly used for overcasting. The newer home sewing machines have lots of fancy stitches. Some of them make overlock and merrow stitches similar the ones you find in manufactured clothing. Any of these could be used for overcasting. Some are only suitable for particular kinds of fabrics. Check your owner's manual for suggestions.

PIPING

Piping is made from cotton cord covered with bias fabric. It is inserted in seams for dec-

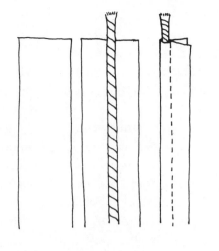

Piping construction

oration and to add stability to the seams. To make your own piping, cut a piece of cord that is slightly longer than needed.

Beginning at one end, cover the cord with the bias strip by folding the bias in half lengthwise over it. Match the two long raw edges of the bias. Pin the bias over the cording in this manner for the entire length of the cord.

Stitch the bias strip close to the cording using the zipper foot on your machine.

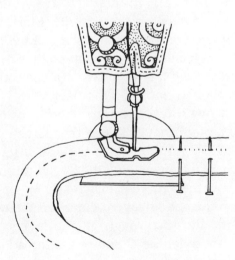

Stitching the piping with a zipper foot

RUFFLES

You can add a ruffle to almost any edge to fancy things up a bit. It can be any length you decide looks good. When making your own ruffles, design them to suit the individual project. Make them very slightly shirred, or tightly gathered for a dramatic fussy effect.

Already-ruffled fabric and laces are often available in stores.

Ruffles can be inserted into a seam or applied to a hemmed edge from the wrong side. They look very good when put around curved edges such as on a round pillow.

The best looking ruffles are made from bias fabric. They fall softly and gather well easily. Use 2"-wide bias hem facing to make contrasting ruffles. Press the turned-under edges of the tape out flat. Press the bias in half lengthwise, matching the raw edges. Gather along these raw edges. Apply the ruffle so the gathering stitches don't show. The ends of the ruffle can be hemmed as in Project One or by merely turning the raw ends of the ruffle into the seam or under the edge.

SEAM GUIDES

There are several types of seam guides. They all serve the same purpose. You place the edge of your fabric against the edge of the seam guide so that your seam allowances are all equal. They are very helpful for sewing a larger-than-normal seam allowance.

A seam guide may have come with the attachments to your machine. These screw on to your machine. Look at the throat plate (sometimes called the needle plate) on your machine. It should have lines etched in the metal that are labeled for several different size seam allowances.

You can get a small magnetic seam guide in a notions department. Check your machine to be sure the magnet will adhere to it. If the flatbed of the machine is plastic or aluminum alloy, the magnet won't adhere to it.

You can easily make your own seam guide

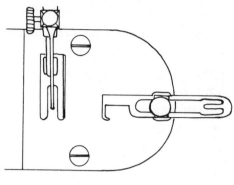

Seam guide

with a piece of colored tape. Place a ruler under the needle. Rotate the wheel so that the needle gently rests on any inch mark. Place the tape on the flatbed of the machine so that it indicates any seam allowance width you want. The fabric edge is aligned with the edge of the tape during sewing. A ½" seam allowance is used for all the projects in this book. If you are not accustomed to sewing with a ½" seam allowance, be sure to mark it on your machine with some type of seam guide.

TRIMMING SEAM ALLOWANCES

Seams often overlap when pieces of fabric are joined together, especially in patchwork. This overlapping of layers can cause bumps and ridges on the right side of your work. Often these bumps and ridges don't show up until it is pressed, worn, or laundered. To eliminate this problem, remember to trim the seam allowances.

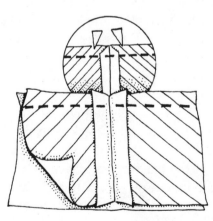

Trimming seam ends diagonally

When one seam rests exactly on top of another, trim one of the seams so that that seam allowance is narrower than the other. The seam closest to the outside or right side of the project should have the largest seam allowance. The seam toward the inside should be trimmed down. In this way, several layers of fabric do not stop abruptly in one spot. When trimmed in this step-like way, seam allowances are rarely visible.

Trim the ends of any seam allowances diagonally when they are outside the stitching. This prevents a bump at the intersection of two seams.

TUFTING

This is a way of fastening quilt batting between two layers of cloth. It is done by tying rather than stitching. Some upholstery is tufted and so are many comforters.

The ties are spaced as closely as you like. If you are using many layers of batting, and the piece is very thick, the tufting should be done more closely together. This prevents the layers from shifting and separating. Often during use or washing, batting will lump or knot up inside if it is not tufted sufficiently.

Make sure all the layers are evenly smoothed out before you begin. Mark the spots where you plan to make a tuft by pinning through all the layers on the right side. If you are making a large piece or a comforter, spread your work out on the floor.

Use heavy thread, yarn, or crochet cotton. Thread a piece about 12" long on a large-eyed needle. Holding the needle vertical, insert it through all the layers. Pull the thread through until about a 4" end remains. Take a ⅛" or ¼" stitch on the bottom layer, and insert the needle vertically up through all the layers. Be careful not to let the 4" end of the thread slip through the fabric.

Insert the needle down again at the first spot next to the 4" end. Pull the thread through to the underside. This security stitch should squeeze the three layers together

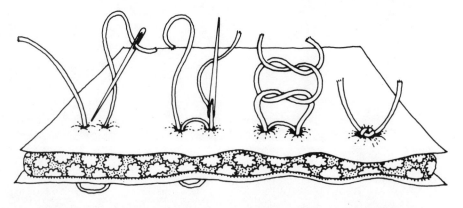

A: The first stitch B: The security stitch C: The square knot D: Completed tuft

snugly. Return the thread to the top as you did before.

Pull the two ends gently. Tie a square knot closely against the fabric. Clip the thread ends to about ½" to 1" long.

For a special decorative effect, string a bead or button onto the second underside stitch. This then becomes the right side of the piece so begin working from the wrong side.

ZIPPER SHORTENING

Zippers are sold in standard lengths. Stores do not always stock every length made. Whatever the reason, it is necessary to shorten a zipper once in a while.

Buy a zipper larger than you need. Close the zipper. At the top where the pull stops, there is a metal "stop" that keeps the pull from going right off the zipper. Measure from this "stop" down the zipper teeth. Mark the *new* zipper length by drawing a line across both sides of the zipper tape. This will become the new bottom of the zipper teeth.

A new bottom stop must be made at this mark. It is not impossible to move the original stop up to the new location; however, it takes an ice pick, a pair of pliers, and very strong, nimble fingers to do it.

I recommend making a new stop at the new zipper bottom as follows. Thread a needle with thread that matches the zipper. Knot both ends together so that you are working with a double thread. Insert your needle from the wrong side into the zipper tape at the mark. It should be right next to the teeth. Take a stitch over the teeth, and insert the needle into the zipper tape at the mark on the other side. Repeat this stitch around the zipper teeth until you have made a stop out of thread.

Test your stop by unzipping the zipper. The pull should not go past your thread stop. Cut the zipper off about ¾" below your stop. You can remove the teeth below the stop by pulling them out with a pair of pliers. This is not necessary to do unless the teeth are very raised and will show through the fabric when the zipper is inserted.

A second method of making a stop can be used on plastic or nylon zippers. Mark the new length as with the first method. Slowly sew back and forth over the mark by machine several times. Be careful not to break the machine needle on the teeth. The needle should slip between the teeth. Cut the excess zipper as before. It is not necessary to remove the excess teeth because plastic zippers are very flat and pliable.

Part
II

SAMPLE BLOCKS AND PROJECTS TO MAKE WITH THEM

CHAPTER ONE

$\left(\begin{array}{c} Block \\ 1 \end{array}\right)$ Basic Quilting

Probably most of the quilting you have seen is the type called plain or basic quilting. Besides its beautiful, decorative appearance, it also has a very practical side. Quilting provides warmth, as in a ski parka; insulation, as in an oven mitt; and protection, as in a placemat. This technique also adds strength, stiffness, and durability to any fabric.

A soft batting or filler is sandwiched between two pieces of cloth. These three layers are then secured together by stitching. The stitching usually follows a design or pattern. This quilting design is drawn on the fabric, and the stitches are made on top of these lines.

Quilting can be done either by hand or by machine. The hand sewing stitch used is called a running stitch. The smaller your stitches, the finer and more durable the work. The space between each stitch should be the same length as the stitch itself. The finished stitching forms a decorative relief surface that resembles embossing. It is completely reversible because the stitches are the same on both sides, and the knots are neatly hidden.

For this basic quilting sample block you will use a cotton scarf, handkerchief, or bandana. Choose one you like for its special color, pattern, or design. Working by hand or with a machine, you outline or repeat the shape of the printed design with quilting stitches. Using techniques called "outlined" and "echo" quilting, you transform the scarf design into a lively dimpled square.

Supplies (enough for one sample block)

15″ square cotton scarf, handkerchief, or bandana

    Select something with a printed design in a color that you like. If the scarf is larger than 15″ x 15″ square, see the directions below. You also may cut a 15″ square from yard goods or an old tablecloth with a design printed in the center of it.

½ yard of muslin

½ yard of polyester fleece

    You may substitute one or two layers of soft flannel.

Thread

    Choose a color that accents or contrasts well with the scarf. It will be used for quilting.

DIRECTIONS

Cutting:

Take out the hem from the 15″ scarf by carefully removing the stitching. If the scarf is larger than 15″ square, trim off an equal amount of fabric on all four sides so that it measures exactly 15″ x 15″, and the design is centered on the square. If you are using yard goods or a tablecloth with a large printed pattern, try to position the square so that one printed motif, such as a flower, is located in the center of the square. Use the L square to straighten and square off the 15″ x 15″ piece. Cut a 15″ square from the muslin backing fabric and the fleece, using the scarf as a pattern.

Quilting the three layers:

Smooth the muslin square out on a flat surface. Put the fleece square on top of the muslin. Place the scarf directly on top of the fleece with the right side up (Figure 1). Match the corners and raw edges of all three pieces, making sure they are all flat. Pin them together along the outer edges at one inch intervals, and baste all of the squares together ½″ from the raw edges.

Baste a large X across the block from corner to corner. This basting will prevent any of the layers from shifting when you do the quilting (Figure 2).

The block is now ready to quilt. Your quilting design should compliment the printed design of the fabric.

FIGURE 1:
The three layers of
the quilted block

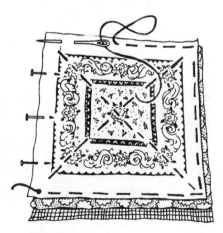

FIGURE 2:
Basting the three
layers together

Analyze the printed design and decide how the scarf should be quilted. Select a simple quilting diagram that will enhance the printed design. See Figure 3 for suggestions on how to quilt your block.

The top diagram (A) in Figure 3 illustrates echo quilting. The rows of stitching surround and move out from a central motif like ripples made by dropping a stone into water. Spaces between each row of stitching can be equal, or they can increase or decrease gradually as they get further from the central motif. This design resembles concentric circles, as in a target.

The second diagram (B) is a sunburst extending out from one row of outline stitching. This diagram looks equally well if the radiating lines are drawn at random or if they are geometrically perfect in their spacing.

The most common of all is the lower diagram (C). It uses a grid pattern of stitching. This pattern is best if you have chosen fabric that has an all-over design. If you are using gingham fabric, your stitches will follow or intersect the lines of the woven checks evenly. The grid pattern can also be used diagonally, forming diamonds rather than squares.

If you are doing outline quilting, make all the outline stitches first, and then fill in the surrounding or background areas with either an echo, sunburst, or grid pattern. The combinations of quilting patterns that you can make are endless. Select the ones that you like best for your own particular fabric. If your fabric is very plain, you can combine several patterns for a more complex quilting diagram. If your fabric has a busy printed design on it, less quilting is fine.

For quilting a small piece such as this, plan the quilting lines directly on the fabric. Use your clear ruler and straight pins to experiment, mark, and space quilting lines. Position the pins in lines as though they were stitching. This way you can visualize the quilting diagram before you stitch it. If you don't like one diagram, try another.

When you have decided on the quilting diagram that you like most, draw the lines lightly on the fabric. Use a soft marking pencil or chalk in a contrasting color that can be brushed or washed away later. Make sure that it is water soluble.

The quilting stitches will fall directly on the drawn lines. Use the running stitch for hand quilting. Take several stitches on your needle at a time. Make sure that

FIGURE 3:

A: Echo quilting diagram

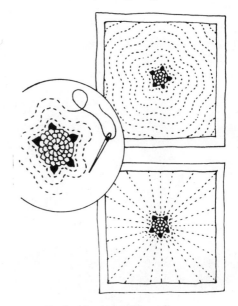

B: Sunburst quilting diagram

C: Grid pattern quilting diagram

each stitch goes completely through all three layers to the muslin side. Pull the stitches taut but not tight. The stitches should sink into the fabric and pinch all three layers together. Your stitching should not gather the three layers. (See Quilting Stitch, p. 32.) It should lie flat and not look squeezed up.

Your finished quilted block may measure slightly smaller than 15" x 15". This is because the quilting has a tendency to draw in the fabric. Do not be alarmed by a slight difference in size. Only if you are making quilted fabric for fitted clothing do you need to be concerned about the amount of quilting shrinkage that will occur by this drawing up.

Make your knots on the muslin side. This side will not show when you use the block to make a project.

The block can be quilted by machine if you prefer. It is faster, but it does not have the soft look of beautiful hand quilting.

To machine quilt, make lines of machine stitches over the lines of the quilting diagram as in hand stitching. Machine quilting is fast. It has a more defined, linear appearance than that of hand quilting.

Prepare the top, filler and backing layers, and mark the quilting diagram in the same way as for hand quilting. Be sure to pin and baste the three layers together very well. The more preliminary basting that you do, the better your final results will be. Basting thoroughly also makes it much easier to machine quilt. The machine quilts much faster than you can by hand so it is more difficult to prevent the layers from shifting.

The stitch length should be between six and ten stitches per inch. The thicker the batting, or the more slippery the top fabric, the larger the stitch length should be.

A quilting foot attachment for your machine can be very helpful for making straight, evenly spaced rows of quilting. It has a guide on it that allows you to make parallel rows of machine quilting without marking each row with chalk lines. Check the owner's manual for instructions on using a quilting foot on your machine.

Feed the right side of the quilting under the foot of your machine. Lessen the presser foot pressure if you can to allow the thick quilting to feed easily under the presser foot. Hold your hands on either side of the needle. Gently pull outward toward the sides and slightly back as the machine stitches. Remove any pins as you go. Work slowly at first until you are sure of the technique. To prevent tucks, gradually ease in any extra fullness occurring in the top fabric as you procede.

When you stop stitching anywhere in the quilting diagram, to refill a bobbin or for whatever reason, pull the ends of the threads through to the muslin side and knot them to prevent unraveling. (See Knotting the Ends of Your Threads, p. 38.)

Use this quilted block to construct Project 1: An Ace of an Apron or for any other project in the book.

The soft look of quilting lends itself to almost any type of garment. Use it as an entire garment or as accents such as cuffs and collar. Many household items, such as oven mitts, appliance covers, and placemats, are quilted. It is a beautiful as well as functional technique. A quilted block is a good way to cover an old chair seat or extend the life of jackets and sweaters by adding quilted elbow patches.

$\widehat{Project\ 1}$ An Ace of an Apron

The project in this chapter uses *one* quilted sample block. The quilted scarf in this chapter, or any other sample block that has been quilted, becomes the bib of an apron that you can make for any member of the family.

SUPPLIES

One quilted sample block

1¼ yards of 44″ or 45″ wide printed cotton or cotton-blend fabric

> Pick out something that matches or blends well with the scarf or quilted block that you are using for the bib. It will be used for the skirt and the ruffle of the apron.

¾ yard of 44″ or 45″ wide broadcloth

> Choose a solid color that accents or contrasts with the quilted block and the skirt fabric. It will be used for the block lining, the neck string, and the two waist ties.

1½ yards of jumbo rickrack, piping, or ruffled trim
> This should match the thread and the broadcloth if possible.

Thread
> It should match the contrasting broadcloth.

DIRECTIONS

The apron can be made in three sizes—small, medium, and large. Changes for medium and large sizes will be found in parenthesis.

Cutting:

Cut all pieces so that their longest measurements are placed on the crossgrain of the fabrics.

From the 1¼ yard skirt fabric, cut a rectangle that measures 32″ x 20″ (Medium 34″ x 22″, Large 36″ x 24″). Cut out two pieces from the same fabric that measure 9″ x 36″ (Medium 9″ x 40″, Large 9″ x 44″). These are for the ruffle. If you are making the large size apron, and your fabric is slightly narrower than 45″, cut the ruffle pieces as long as possible. Don't worry if the pieces are 43″ or even 42″ across. A few less inches of fabric will not be noticeable in the gathered ruffle when it is put on the apron.

From the ¾ yard of contrasting broadcloth, cut two pieces on the crosswise grain for the waist ties that measure 2″ x 25″ (Medium 2″ x 27″, Large 2″ x 29″). Cut two pieces that measure 2″ x 28″ (Medium 2″ x 30″, Large 2″ x 32″). These will be joined together to make the neck string. Cut another piece that measures 15″ x 15″ from the same fabric. This is the block lining.

Lining the block:

Place the quilted block down flat with the right side up. Put the 15″ square of lining on top. Match the raw edges and pin the pieces together. Baste them together ½″ from the raw edges (Figure 4A). Leave a 6″ unstitched opening in the center of one side. Go over your basting by machine. If you are working by hand, all machine stitching can be substituted with the backstitch (Figure 4B).

To eliminate unwanted thickness at the edges of the quilted block, you will need to grade the seams. Trim the block and the lining to ¼″. Trim the fleece and the muslin to ⅛″. Do not trim along the 6″ opening at all.

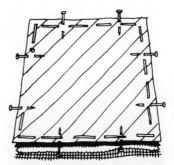

FIGURE 4:
A: *Pinning and basting the quilted block to the lining*

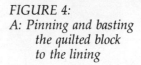
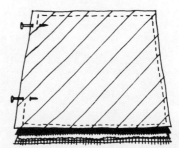

B: *Machine stitching the lining to the quilted scarf leaving a 6″ opening on one side*

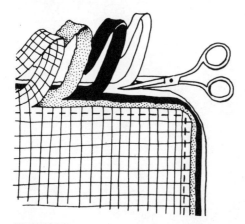

FIGURE 5:
Trimming the different layers and corners by a process called grading

FIGURE 6:
The basted bib foldline is at the top of the illustration. The rickrack is basted to the edge beginning and ending 1" above the bib foldline

Trim the four corners of all the fabrics carefully, rounding them to about an ⅛" from the machine stitching. This prevents the corner from being lumpy after it is turned inside (Figure 5).

Reach into the 6" opening and turn the right side of the scarf to the outside. The muslin will not be visible; it will be concealed by the lining. Tuck in the seam allowance along the 6" opening, and baste the edges closed evenly. Flatten the seam edges on all four sides of the block by rolling them between your fingers and pressing. Press the entire block flat so that the lining fabric cannot be seen on the scarf side.

Applying the rickrack to the bib:

Holding the quilted scarf in a diamond position, decide what corner of the design should be at the top of the apron. Measure 3" from this top corner along the edge of the scarf to both the left and right sides. Mark these points with pins. Using a ruler and marking pencil, connect these two points by drawing a line on the lining side. This portion of the bib is later folded back at the top neck edge of the apron to make a casing for the neck string. Mark this line with white basting stitches (Figure 6).

The rickrack is now applied to all sides of the block beginning and ending 1" above the bib foldline. Pin and baste the rickrack under the edges so that only half of it is visible on the right side of the block. Attach the piping or ruffled trim in the same way. Baste it ⅛" away from the edge of the scarf so that it is fastened securely in place (Figure 6).

Hemming the apron skirt:

Hem the long top side and two short sides of the rectangle for the skirt section, as follows: First, press under ¼" toward the wrong side of the fabric. Turn over ¼" once again and pin in place. Miter the corners. (See Mitering Hems, p. 39.) Stitch the hem in place by hand or machine (Figure 7).

Joining the bib and the skirt sections together:

Fold the skirt section in half so that the shorter two hemmed edges match. Crease the center fold with the iron, and then open it out flat. With all right sides up, position the quilted block over the skirt section so that the bib foldline is toward the top. Center the bottom corner of the scarf on the crease line. The left and right corners of the block must meet the long hemmed top edge of the skirt section. Pin this and baste it securely in place (Figure 8).

Machine stitch around the entire block ⅛" from the seamed edge (over the basting), securing the rickrack to the scarf and the block to the skirt at the same time. Begin stitching at the top corner above the bib foldline where the rickrack begins. This also closes the opening in the block where you turned it right side out.

The skirt ruffle:

The ruffle is made up of two pieces that are sewn together forming a seam at the center of the ruffle. Place the two pieces together with the right sides facing each other. Seam them together along one of the short 9" sides using a ½" seam allowance (Figure 9). Press this seam open.

Then fold the ruffle in half lengthwise with the right sides inside. Match the short ends. Stitch them together from the top to bottom, that is, from the raw edges to

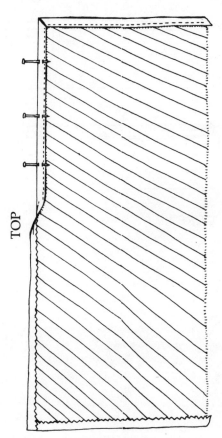

FIGURE 7: Hemming the top and sides of the skirt section. Notice the mitered corner

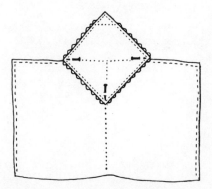

FIGURE 8: Positioning the bib on the hemmed skirt section

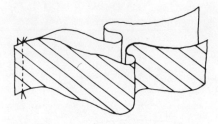

FIGURE 9: Joining the two pieces of the ruffle

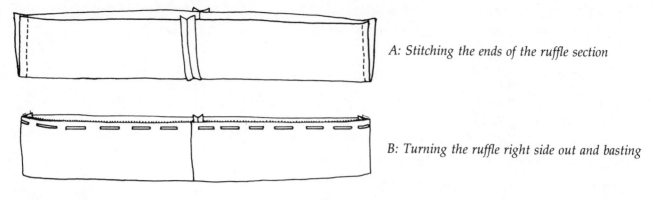

A: Stitching the ends of the ruffle section

B: Turning the ruffle right side out and basting

FIGURE 10:

the fold. You now have a long canoe-shaped piece (Figure 10A). Trim the seam allowance to ¼". Turn this canoe shape right side out. Flatten and press the end seams flat. Match the long raw edges of the ruffle pieces and press a crease where the ruffle folds exactly in half lengthwise. This is the lower finished hem edge of the ruffle. Pin and baste the two raw edges together (Figure 10B).

Gather along the raw edges of the ruffle by hand or by machine (See Gathering, p. 37.) Distribute the fullness evenly until the gathered edge of the ruffle is the same length as the unhemmed long edge of the skirt.

Press under ½" on the unhemmed edge of the skirt section (Figure 11). Position and pin this edge over the gathered ruffle so that the gathering threads are not visible.

On the right side, pin, baste, and then topstitch by machine close to the turned edge. Topstitch again approximately ¼" above the first row of stitching, securing

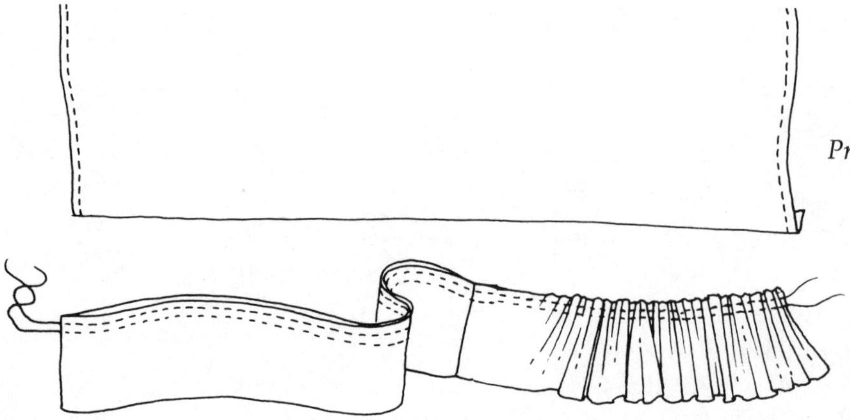

FIGURE 11:

Pressing under unhemmed skirt edge

Gathering the ruffle to the same length as the skirt section.

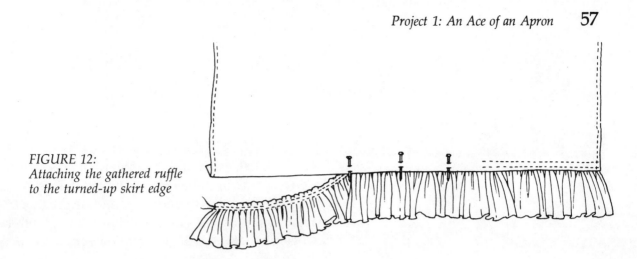

FIGURE 12:
*Attaching the gathered ruffle
to the turned-up skirt edge*

the ruffle down flat to the skirt section. Do not stretch the skirt section while stitching (Figure 12).

The neck string and two waist ties:

Sew the two pieces of the neck string (2" x 28") together at the 2" ends to make one long piece. Press the seam open. Press under ½" on the two remaining 2" ends (Figure 13A). Press under ½" on all four of the 2" ends of the waist ties (Figure 13B). Fold the neck string in half lengthwise with the right sides facing each other (Figure 14A). The ends should be even where you pressed the ½" under. Pin the long raw edges together. Stitch the long raw edges together using a ½" seam allowance. Secure the ½" ends that you pressed under (Figure 14B). Trim the seam allowance to ¼". Insert a small safety pin into the seam allowance close to the seam at one end. Poke the closed pin into the open short end of the tie and push it through the inside for the entire length of the tie (Figure 14C). The finished tie will be ½" wide.

Working on an ironing board, flatten the seam edge of each tie by rolling it between your fingers. Press the ties flat. Topstitch ⅛" away from the seam edges and the folded edge. The edgestitching makes the ties flat. It also makes them stronger and more durable. Stitch the two remaining waist ties in the same manner.

Attaching the waist ties:

Position each of the two waist ties to the skirt section on the right side of the fabric, at the outermost corners of the rectangle. The seams of the waist ties should be

FIGURE 13:

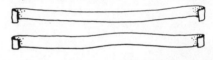

A: *Seaming the neck string,
and pressing under ½"
on the ends*

B: *Pressing under ½" on all four ends
of the two waist ties*

FIGURE 14:

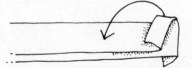

A: *½" end pressed under*

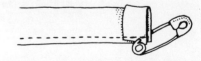

B: *Folding the ties in half lengthwise*

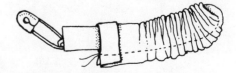

C: *Stitching the ties. Inserting a safety pin
in the seam allowance of one end*

D: *Turning the tie right side out*

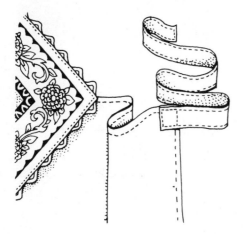

FIGURE 15:
Attaching the ties to the skirt section

directed toward the hem of the skirt. Pin them in position, and stitch in a small square to fasten them in place securely (Figure 15).

Attaching the neck string:

Working flat, position the center of the neck string on the wrong side of the block just below the bib foldline. Crease the bib at the foldline. Pin and secure this folded triangle to the wrong side of the block lining with hand stitches. Do not catch the neck string with your stitches. It should slide back and forth easily. Also hand stitch the top of the skirt section to the wrong side of the bib between the side corners so that it lies flat (Figure 16).

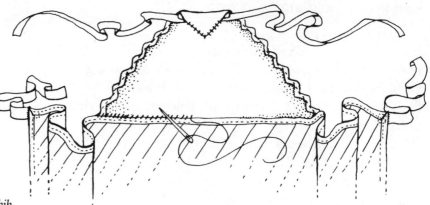

FIGURE 16:
Hand stitching the back of the bib at the neck edge and the waist

SUGGESTIONS

Whether you are a beginner or have been sewing for years, you may want to make changes in the projects for one reason or another. All the projects can easily be made more simple for a beginner or faster if you are just in a hurry.

Any of the blocks given in this book would work equally well for the apron. I have made it over and over again. It can be made very fussy and feminine, or plain, or even masculine. The basic shapes are easy to adapt to any "look" that you're after by merely changing the block, the colors, the trims, or the fabric. Subtract the ruffle and add pockets for a whole new look.

The block used for the bib should be quilted to give body to the apron. It also makes a sort of pot holder for the front of you that absorbs splashes and insulates if you're up against the stove a lot.

If you use any of the blocks given in Chapter Fourteen, make sure to place the design on the square diagonally. The Picture Appliqué will then be upright when the apron bib is used diagonally.

SIMPLIFICATIONS

Ruffle: The ruffle at the hem of the apron can be eliminated entirely if you are making the apron for your chef, or if you just can't stand ruffles. Put a plain hem at the bottom edge of the skirt section in the same way that you hemmed the other three sides. Miter the lower corners just like the upper corners of the skirt section.

Instead of making your own ruffle, you can buy pretty, wide lace or eyelet that is already gathered. Get one yard. Stitch it to the skirt by following the instructions given for attaching the ruffle.

Rickrack: The rickrack trim around the bib section could be eliminated if you like. Merely construct the apron in the same manner skipping the section on applying rickrack. Other types of trimming, such as piping, lace, or gathered eyelet could also be used in place of the rickrack if you prefer.

Neck string and waist ties: Making your own neck string and waist ties from fabric is a very special touch. You can use ribbon to save time. Find some ½" wide satin or grosgrain ribbon in a color you like. You will need 3 yards. Cut it to the following lengths:

one neck string, 55" (Medium 57", Large 59")

waist ties, 24" (Medium 26", Large 28")

Bias tape 1" wide could also be substituted as the neck string and waist ties. Cut it to the same lengths as given above. Press under ½" on all the short ends. Fold the bias tape in half lengthwise and topstitch the long edges together. The finished ties will be ½" wide. Attach the ribbon or bias tape to the skirt section exactly as shown for making your own ties.

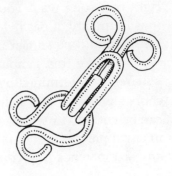

CHAPTER TWO

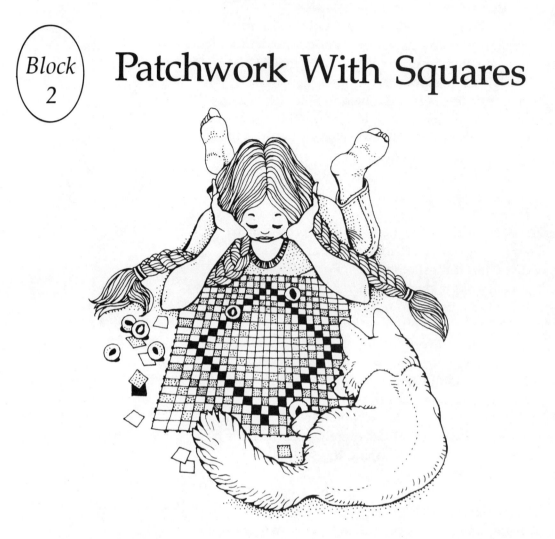

Block 2 — Patchwork With Squares

Patchwork using squares is one of the most common because it is the most simple to do. It follows the same basic construction that all other forms of patchwork do. Many small pieces of different colored fabrics are joined together by seams. This results in a large piece that is one layer of fabric throughout, except for the seam allowances.

Patchwork from squares is very versatile because it works equally well with all types of fabrics. The wide selection of printed fabrics and colors that are available to you make it easy and fun to assemble a block. You cannot fail by planning your own color scheme because there is no right or wrong way. You select the fabrics and arrange them however you like. Because of the mosaic quality of patchwork, any combination that you like will be a success. The fabrics that you select should be similar in thickness and weight so that the finished patchwork lies flat.

To make this sample block, you will use squares that are all the same size. The size of the squares is determined by how you want the finished piece to look. The type of fabric that you choose will give you a clue to what size squares are best. Medium weight, firmly woven fabrics can be cut into tiny pieces easily. Very light weight or very thick fabrics are not as easy to manage in small pieces. If your fabric frays easily, stick to larger squares. Just as with the color selection, any size patches that you feel comfortable working with will look fine. This technique is a good one for recycling scraps or old clothing. If you are using up your old scrap fabrics, consider the general size of the scraps to make sure that they are large enough to cut out the squares that you want.

Larger squares are more simple to work with, and the assembling is quicker; however, the designs and color arrangements achieved by using smaller squares are well worth any additional time and trouble. The procedure is exactly the same for either large or small squares.

SUPPLIES *(enough for two sample blocks)*

Scrap fabrics

> Approximately one yard of assorted fabrics you like. These should be similar in weight and composition for the best results. The easiest types to work with are broadcloth and cotton blend fabrics. If you want to do a special planned color design, you will need to buy new fabrics. See Estimating Yardage, p. 23, for determining how much fabric you will need.

Thread

> Select one color thread that blends well with all the fabrics you are using. It is not necessary to change your thread color to match each different color of fabric. The thread becomes almost invisible within the seam after stitching. If you are using many different colors, use thread that blends with the overall tone of the fabrics. Use black for darks, beige for mediums, and white for lights.

DIRECTIONS

Planning:

You will be designing this block yourself. Spend some time deciding what type of fabrics you would like to use. You also can select the size of the squares, the colors of the fabric, and the arrangement of the squares. It's easy to make this sample block over and over again and never have two blocks look the same.

If you plan a design using printed fabrics or certain color squares that will be repeated, make a small, quick sketch first. Use graph paper and crayons or colored pencils to plan the design before you begin working. This way, you can quickly determine how many squares are needed in each color. This is also the best way to experiment and determine what arrangement of color is best. Keep your sketch handy to refer to while sewing the squares together.

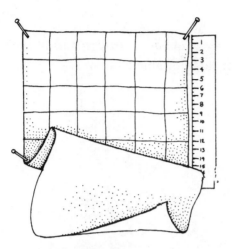

FIGURE 1:
Drawing a grid on the fabric

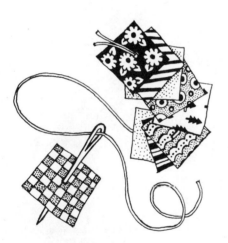

FIGURE 2:
String patches to keep them together

Cutting:

The cutting measurements of the different size squares are shown in the chart below. Select *one* size square from the six that are given. Make a cardboard template that is the same as the *cutting size* for your square. A ½" seam allowance is included on all sides of each square.

Use the cardboard template as a pattern. Lay each piece of fabric out flat. Place the template on the fabric so that one side of the square is even with the straightened edge of the fabric. Hold the template in position with one hand and draw around it with a pencil or chalk.

If you need to cut many squares from one piece of fabric, draw a grid right on the fabric. Using a ruler and pencil, draw a grid in which the spaces between the lines are the same as the *cutting size* that is given for your square. The lines of the grid should run parallel with the grain of the fabric (Figure 1).

Cut the fabric squares out on the lines you have drawn. To keep the squares together, string them on thread like beads. This will keep them neat and handy when you need them (Figure 2). If you are doing a large number of squares in each color, string the squares in the same color fabric separately.

CUTTING CHART

Cutting Size	Number of Squares Needed	Finished Size After Sewing	Number of Squares in Each Row
8"x 8"	4	7"x 7"	2
5⅝"x 5⅝"	9	4⅝"x 4⅝"	3*
4½"x 4½"	16	3½"x 3½"	4
3"x 3"	49	2"x 2"	7
2¾"x 2¾"	64	1¾"x 1¾"	8
2"x 2"	196	1"x 1"	14

Assembling the patchwork:

The finished sample block when all the squares are seamed together is 15" square. This includes a ½" seam allowance on all four sides. The method for assembling the block is the same for any *number* of squares in any *size* that you have selected from the cutting chart.

If you are not working from a color sketch, lay all the squares out on a table with their right sides up. Check the cutting chart for the number of squares in each row. Lay out the entire block as it will appear after sewing. Move the squares around until you are satisfied with the arrangement. Some fabrics have a one-way design, such as trees, flowers and animals, and may need to be placed in a certain direction (Figure 3).

When you have decided on the placement, number the squares lightly on the wrong side. In this way, you can put them away before they are all sewn together without mixing them up. If you are using a color sketch, number the squares on it, and keep it handy to check the proper position of each color.

Begin with the top row. Pin the first two squares together using a ½″ seam allowance. Always put the right sides together. Use the backstitch if you are working by hand (Figure 4A). Complete the entire row by joining the remaining squares in the same way. Press all the seams open (Figure 4B).

Complete all the rows of squares. Put each row in its place on the table as you finish it.

Next, join the rows of squares together. Pin the first row to the second using a ½″ seam allowance. Match the seams of the squares as closely as possible. Baste this seam to prevent the matched seams from moving (Figure 4C). Stitch all the rows of squares together. Trim the intersections of the seams diagonally to eliminate bulkiness (see Trimming Seam Allowances, p. 42). Press the seams open.

The block is now ready to be used for the project in this chapter, A Pushover of a Pillow.

If you would like to quilt this block, refer to Block 1 for quilting directions. A good quilting diagram for this block would be X's or O's in each square. Other diagrams, such as a simple daisy, could be stitched in every other square. Tufting looks very good on this type of patchwork (see Tufting, p. 42).

This method of assembly is used for joining all types of squares together. It is a technique that you will be using over and over again.

*A finished block made of 5⅝″ squares will measure 13⅞″. The ⅛″ difference won't be significant when the block is used in a project.

FIGURE 3:
Arranging the squares

FIGURE 4:

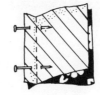

A: *Seaming the first two squares together*

B: *Seaming the first row together*

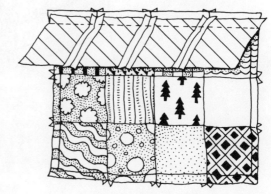

C: *Seaming the rows together*

Project
2

A Pushover of a Pillow

The project in this chapter uses *one* sample block. The patchwork sample block in this chapter or any other sample block is used for the front of a pillow that will look at home anywhere you put it.

SUPPLIES

One quilted or unquilted sample block

1 yard of solid color fabric

> Pick a color that goes well with the block you are using for the front of the pillow. It will be used for the piping and the back of the pillow. Sailcloth, corduroy, velveteen, and lightweight canvas are all suitable. Get something that looks good and wears well.

12″ dress zipper

> It should be the same color as the solid color fabric. If you can't find a 12″ zipper, you can cut down a longer zipper if necessary (see Zipper Shortening, p. 43).

Pillow filler

> Use a 14″ foam square insert, or make your own muslin pillow filled with polyester fiber filler.

2 yards of piping

DIRECTIONS

Cutting:

To prepare the back of the pillow, cut the following pieces from the pillow fabric:

> **a** 15″ x 7½″
> **b** 15″ x 9½″

Inserting the zipper:

Match the two 15″ edges of sections **a** and **b**. Mark a seam line 1″ from the raw edge. Baste the two sections together along the seamline. Measure in 1½″ from *both* ends of the seamline. Make a mark on each side. Machine stitch the sections together from the side edges in toward the marks. Secure the stitching at the marks. Leave the seamline unstitched between the marks except for the basting. The length of the unstitched section is equal to the length of your zipper (12″) (Figure 5A). Press the seam open.

Place the combined pieces flat on a table with the right side up. Fold **a** (the smaller one) down over **b**. Press a crease in the seam allowance of **b** that is ⅛″ away from the seamline.

Pin and baste the zipper tape next to this fold with the crease ⅛″ away from the zipper teeth. Make sure the zipper is positioned within the opening that is only basted closed. When the basting is removed, the zipper

FIGURE 5:

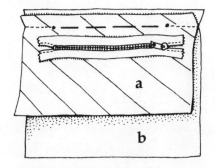

A: Sewing the two back sections together, leaving a zipper opening

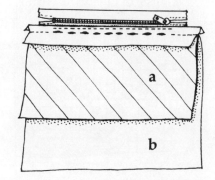

B: Stitching the lower tape of the zipper to the seam allowance of section **b**

will fill the unstitched section on the seamline.

Stitch by machine ⅛" from the crease line using a zipper foot (Figure 5B). Press **a** up into its original position. Pin and baste **a** to the zipper tape ⅝" away from crease line. Stitch along the basting line by machine across the entire width of the block (Figure 6). Remove the bastings.

Applying the piping:

Put the completed pillow back with the zipper aside. Next, you will prepare the pillow front by applying piping. Piping is a professional looking way to finish the edge of the pillow. It lends support and provides strength and durability to a pillow that is sure to get lots of use.

Cut or make a 58" length of piping. You can buy packaged piping in many colors. If you want to make your own piping in matching fabric, see Piping, p. 40. Leave about 4" of the piping unstitched at both ends.

If you are using packaged piping, cut a 58" length. Remove the stitching at both ends for about 4", exposing the cording inside (Figure 7).

Find the center of the piping (29" from one end) by folding it in half. Begin applying it by placing the center point at the middle of the top side of the sample block you are using for the front of the pillow. Match the raw edges of the piping with the raw edge of the block. Pin the piping around the block so that the stitching that holds the piping together is ½" from the raw edge of the block. Clip the seam allowance of the piping at the corners so that the piping will easily make a nice smooth turn around the square corner.

Pin the piping all around the block until you have reached the middle of the bottom side. Baste the piping in place as you have pinned it (Figure 7). Repeat on the other side of the block.

It is important to make a smooth diagonal seam in the piping so that the two ends don't end abruptly and make an awful bump.

Pull aside the cording inside the piping and flatten out one of the unstitched sections of fabric. Make a mark on the inside of the piping fabric that indicates where the two ends should meet. At this point, make a diagonal crease in one end of the piping fabric that follows the grain of the fabric. Keeping this side flat, make a corresponding crease in the other end of the piping fabric that meets the first diagonal crease.

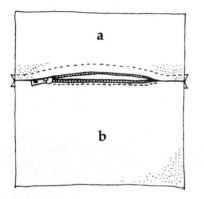

FIGURE 6:
Completing insertion of the zipper
on section **a**

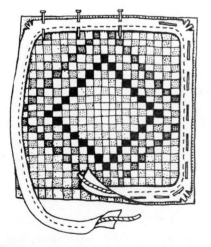

FIGURE 7:
Leaving the two ends of the piping open for 4".
Applying the piping to the front block
of the pillow

Draw a pencil line ½" away from both creases. Cut away the excess fabric on the lines you have drawn. In Figure 8A, the crease is illustrated by a solid line and the cutting line is shown as a dotted line.

Match the crease lines and baste them together. Machine stitch over your basting. Press the seam open. Trim off evenly the corners that extend beyond the edge of the piping fabric (Figure 8B).

Bring the two ends of the cotton cording together at the diagonal seam you have made. Snip off the excess so that they meet exactly. Secure the ends together with a few hand stitches (Figure 8B).

Fold the fabric back in place over the cotton cord. Match the raw edges of the fabric. Baste the fabric together close to the piping (Figure 8C).

Pin and baste this seamed section of piping down to the sample block as you did the rest of the piping.

Joining the pillow sections:

The front and back of the pillow are now ready to be joined together. Place the front of the pillow right side up on a table. Put the back section with the zipper in it on top with the right side down. Make sure the top edges of the two pieces are up. Leave the zipper partially open. Match the raw edges of both squares. Pin and baste the two pieces together using a ½" seam allowance. The stitching should be as close to the piping as possible (Figure 9).

Use a zipper foot to stitch around the entire pillow. The zipper foot can be placed right next to the piping so that you can stitch over your basting right up against it. Trim the corners.

Open the zipper completely. Reach inside the zipper opening and turn the pillow right side out. Insert a 14" x 14" foam pillow insert or a stuffed muslin pillow that you make and stuff yourself from two 15" squares.

SUGGESTIONS

The pillow, like all the other projects, has been demonstrated using some professional finishing techniques. If you are making fifty pillows for the church bazaar, you can take some shortcuts.

Use any one of the sample blocks to make this pillow. Or use all fourteen blocks; what a terrific way to use your sample blocks. You could put them all over the

FIGURE 8:

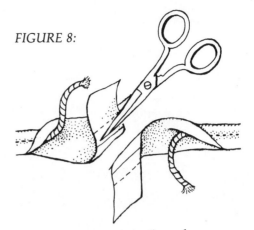

A: Forming the seam in the ends of the piping

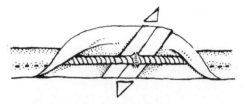

B: Pressing the sewn seam open; trimming the seam allowance; stitching the ends of the cording together

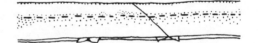

C: The completed seam

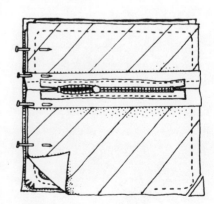

FIGURE 9:
Stitching the front and back of the pillow; trimming corners

house or give them to friends as housewarming presents.

A grouping of two or three different techniques done in the same color scheme could be very effective. Just pick your favorite techniques and your favorite color scheme!

You can use a quilted or unquilted block. It is not necessary to quilt it because it ends up being stuffed. The quilting will perform a decorative function only. Use it if you want to add stitching or subtle texture to the surface.

The pillow could easily be made larger or smaller if you like. Figure any changes in dimensions carefully, especially zipper length. The piping insertion and basic assembling of the pillow are the same for any size or shape pillow. One sample block could be cut diagonally to make two smaller triangular pillows. Four blocks joined together with a tassel on each corner make a fabulous floor pillow. For a less tailored look, put a wide ruffle around the pillow instead of piping.

SIMPLIFICATIONS

Zipper: The zipper is put in so that you can remove the inside pillow and wash or dry clean the cover. If you would like to eliminate it, cut only one back section that measures 15″ x 15″.

Attach it to the front of the pillow in the same way except leave a 6″ opening unstitched on one side of the pillow. Turn the pillow right side out, stuff it and close the opening by hand with the slip stitch.

Piping: The piping is primarily decorative; however, it does give support and stability to the edge of the pillow. The pillow will look nicer and keep its shape longer if it has a piped edge. Heavier fabrics especially do not need as much support, so the piping could be eliminated.

Follow the directions as they are given except eliminate any reference to piping.

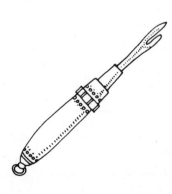

CHAPTER THREE

Block 3

Patchwork With Rectangles

Patchwork with rectangles demonstrates the combination of quilting and patchwork by making a sample block and A Tag-along Tote that you will never get tired of no matter how many times you make it.

This block is made with bright, bold rectangles to give a fresh look to one of the oldest patchwork patterns. You make this intricate looking pattern with shapes that are easy to cut and handle. It is made up of rectangles that are the same width but vary in length. Variations in this design are done with changes in the color arrangement. The rectangles are arranged in a way that results in a block that is divided diagonally by color. The fabrics you use are from two distinct groups, such as light and dark colors, printed and plain fabrics, or as in the case of this project, warm and cool colors of solid fabric.

For the warm colors, choose seven different fabrics that are in the yellow, red, and brown families. For the cool colors, choose six different colors that are greens, blues, purples, and black. The fabrics that you select should have a close or tight weave. They should be similar in weight to each other. Plain broadcloth or cotton is ideal.

SUPPLIES (enough for two sample blocks)

⅛ yard each of seven warm colors
⅛ yard each of six cool colors
½ yard of quilt batting
½ yard of muslin
Black thread

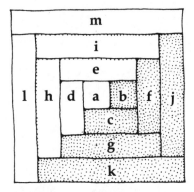

FIGURE 1:
Finished patchwork block showing
diagonal color division

FIGURE 2:

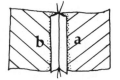

A: Sewing a and b together

B: The seam pressed open

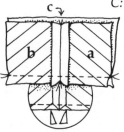

C: Seaming c to a and b;
trimming the seam
diagonally

FIGURE 3:
A: The seams pressed open

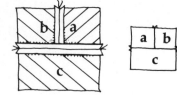

B: Seaming d to the side of a and c

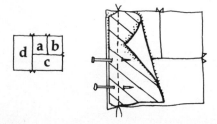

DIRECTIONS

Cutting:

Arrange your warm and cool colors in a sequence from light to dark. The lighter colors should be toward the center of the finished block. Therefore, the smaller pieces are cut from the lighter colors and the larger pieces are cut from the darker colors (Figure 1). You will need one of each of the following:

Warm Colors		Cool Colors	
a	3″ x 3″ (yellow)	**b**	3″ x 3″ (green)
d	3″ x 5″ (gold)	**c**	3″ x 5″ (blue-green)
e	3″ x 7″ (orange)	**f**	3″ x 7″ (blue)
h	3″ x 9″ (red)	**g**	3″ x 9″ (navy)
i	3″ x 11″ (pink)	**j**	3″ x 11″ (purple)
l	3″ x 13″ (maroon)	**k**	3″ x 13″ (black)
m	3″ x 15″ (brown)		

Use a pencil or chalk and a ruler to draw the shapes on the wrong side of the fabric. Position each piece on the fabric so that the straight edge is parallel with the straightened edge or selvage of the fabric. Cut out each piece on the lines you have drawn. Identify each piece by marking the appropriate letter on the wrong side. *Note:* Your fabric colors need not be exactly the same as the ones I have selected. Substitute if you like another color better or if you cannot find a specific color.

Assembling the patchwork:

With the right sides of the fabric facing each other, pin **a** to **b** matching all raw edges. Sew a ½″ seam on one side (Figure 2A). Press the seam open (Figure 2B).

Seam **c** to the bottom of **a** and **b**. Place right sides together, pin ½″ seam, sew, and press open. Clip the

FIGURE 4:
A: Seaming e to the top
of a, b, and d

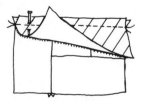

B: a, b, c, d, e assembled

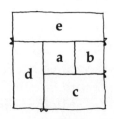

corners of the seam diagonally to the stitching (Figure 2C). This reduces the bulkiness formed when the two seams overlap (Figure 3A).

Seam **d** to the edge of **a** and **c** in the same manner (Figure 3B). Seam **e** to the edge of **a**, **b**, and **d** (Figure 4). Continue to assemble the pieces in this manner in alphabetical order. Looking at the wrong side of the fabric, you will be working in a counterclockwise direction.

Seam **f** to the edge of **e**, **b** and **c**. Seam **g** to **f**, **c**, and **d**. Seam **h** to **g**, **d**, and **e**. Seam **i** to **h**, **e**, and **f**. Seam **j** to **i**, **f**, and **g**. Seam **k** to **j**, **g**, and **h**. Seam **l** to **k**, **h**, and **i**. Seam **m** to **l**, **i**, and **j**. Press all seams open and trim them diagonally.

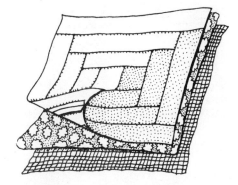

FIGURE 5:
Layering the patchwork block, batting, and muslin

Quilting the patchwork:

Cut a piece of muslin and a piece of quilt batting that measures 15″ square. Place the muslin flat on a table. Put the filler on top of the muslin matching all outer edges. Place the finished block on top with the right side up, facing you (Figure 5). Smooth out all three layers and baste them together along the outer edges. Baste diagonally through the center of the block forming an X as demonstrated in Block 1, Figure 2.

Beginning in the center with the patchwork side facing you, quilt all three layers together by machine. Sew directly on top of the seamline. Sew the seam between **a** and **b** first (Figure 6). Pivot the patchwork at the corner and stitch completely around **a** and **b**. Complete a square until you end where you began. Remove the machine needle, leaving threads about 3″ long, clip and remove the block from the machine (Figure 7). Pull threads through to the muslin side and tie them to pre-

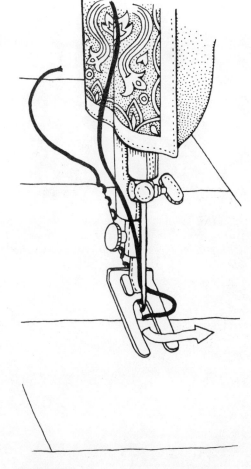

FIGURE 6:
*Machine quilting the seam between **a** and **b**, and preparing to pivot around the corner*

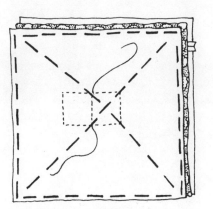

FIGURE 7:
The muslin side of the machine quilting

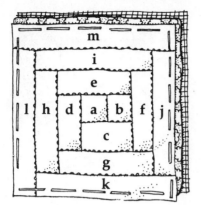

FIGURE 8:
The finished quilted block

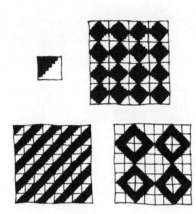

FIGURE 9:
The single block (upper left) can be combined with similar blocks in a variety of layouts. Here are three pattern suggestions

vent unraveling. Repeat this until all the seams are covered with one row of quilting (Figure 8).

You may quilt more than one seam at a time by pivoting the machine needle at corners. Do not go over one seam more than once. Keep the quilting stitches centered on the seamline in order to conceal them between the colored pieces as much as possible. You may like to quilt the block by hand. If so, quilt in the same manner as with machine quilting using the quilting stitch.

The Tag-along Tote in the next part of this chapter requires two quilted blocks. If that's what you plan to do, make a second block the same way you did this one.

This patchwork design is great when you are making something that requires a large number of blocks. The blocks can be combined in a variety of ways that form a larger pattern. This makes especially beautiful quilts! Try some of the combinations and perhaps come up with your *own* arrangement of blocks (Figure 9).

Project
3

A Tag-along Tote

The project in this chapter uses *two* sample blocks that have been quilted. These are used as the sides of an all-purpose tote bag that you will probably never leave behind. It can be washed by machine and is just the right size for carrying small packages, books, and even one full bag of groceries!

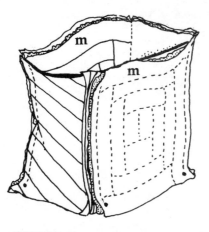

FIGURE 10:
*Seaming the quilted blocks
to the side pieces*

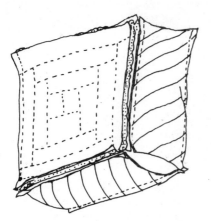

FIGURE 11:
Attaching the bottom

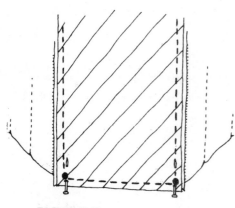

FIGURE 12:
Stitching the ends of the bottom

SUPPLIES

Two quilted sample blocks
1 yard of solid color fabric (44"-45" wide)
> Use lightweight canvas, corduroy, or other heavy-weight fabric. This is for the body of the bag and the handles. The color should blend with the sample block.

1 yard of lining fabric
> Choose a color that won't show the dirt easily.

Cardboard rectangle 5½" x 13½"
> This is inserted to give additional support to the bottom.

Thread
> To match the bag fabric

DIRECTIONS

Cutting:

Cut the following rectangular shapes from the heavy bag fabric.
> two 22" x 4½" (handles)
> three 7" x 15" (bottom and 2 sides)
> one 41" x 4½" (facing for the top edge of the bag)
> Cut from the lining fabric:
> two 15" x 15" (front and back)
> three 7" x 15" (bottom and 2 sides)

Assembling the body of the bag:

Lay the two side pieces and the two quilted blocks out on the table. One side piece should be between the two blocks and the second side piece is to the right side of the block on the right.

If you are using the Patchwork With Rectangles sample blocks, check to be sure that piece **m** is in the top position of each block (Figure 10).

Use ½" seam allowances throughout. Pin and baste the four seams of the body of the bag together. Stitch from the top raw edge down, leaving ½" of each seam unstitched at the bottom of the bag (Figure 10). Secure the ends of your stitching by backtracking.

Turn the bag over and, working from the wrong side, attach the bottom piece to the quilted blocks. The longer sides of the bottom piece are the same length as the blocks. Stitch the bottom to both blocks beginning and ending ½" from the short ends of the bottom piece (Figure 11). Backtrack where the rows of stitches meet one another.

Pin the short end of the bag bottom to the side piece of the bag body. It will fit between the vertical seams that you have already sewn. Put a pin on each side ½" from the edge. Make sure all the other layers underneath are free and will not get caught during stitching. Stitch between the pins (Figure 12). Backtrack where the stitching meets at the corners. This makes the bottom corners of the bag very strong. Repeat on the other end. Turn the bag right side out. Press lightly.

Making the lining:

Assemble the lining in the same manner as the bag. Leave it wrong side out. Insert the finished lining into the bag with the wrong sides together (Figure 13). Pin and baste matching raw edges around the top of the bag (Figure 14).

Making and attaching the handles:

Press under ½" along both long straight edges of the handle pieces. Fold these pieces in half lengthwise. Match, pin, and baste the edges. Machine stitch ⅛" from the matched edges and the folded edges. Topstitch again ¼" from the first row of stitching (Figure 15).

With raw edges together, pin one handle to the top edge of each block. Put the seamed edge toward the center of the bag. The outermost folded edge of the handle piece should be 3" from the side seam. Repeat on the other side. Be sure that the handles are not twisted. Baste them in place (Figure 16).

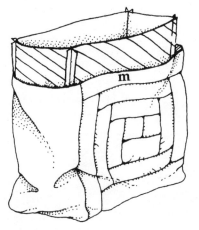

FIGURE 13:
Inserting the lining

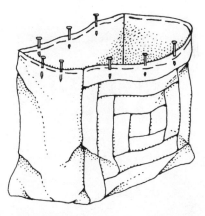

FIGURE 14:
Attaching the lining to the bag

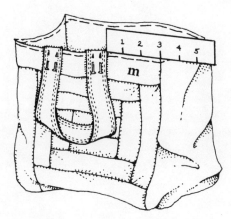

FIGURE 16:
Positioning the handles on the bag

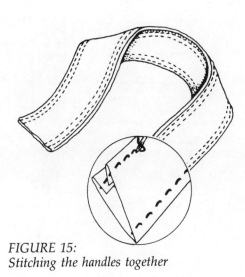

FIGURE 15:
Stitching the handles together

FIGURE 17:

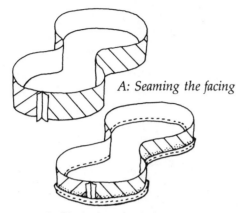

A: Seaming the facing

B: Hemming the facing

Making and attaching the facing:

Sew the two short edges of the facing together with ½″ seam. Press open (Figure 17A). Press under a ½″ hem on one long edge and stitch it down (Figure 17B).

Pin the facing to the bag on the outside matching raw edges. Place the seam in the center of one of the side pieces. Make sure the right sides are together. Sew this seam securely, catching the handles in the seam (Figure 18). Trim and grade this seam to ¼″; open the facing out flat with the seam allowance toward the facing. Machine stitch on the facing ⅛″ from the seam. Stitch the facing and the seam allowances together. This is called understitching a facing, and it helps to keep the facing lying flat inside (Figure 19).

Press the facing to the inside of the bag. Slipstitch the facing by hand to the bag lining (Figure 20).

Place the cardboard rectangle in the bottom of the bag. This will give the bag a flat, rigid bottom. Cover this cardboard with Con-Tact paper if you'd like to make it more durable and easy to clean. Be sure to remove the cardboard bottom when you wash the tote.

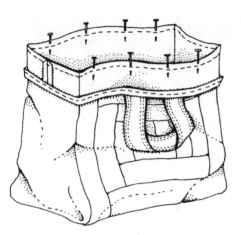

FIGURE 18:
Attaching the facing to the top of the bag

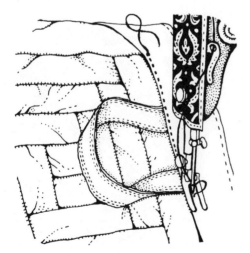

FIGURE 19:
Understitching the facing

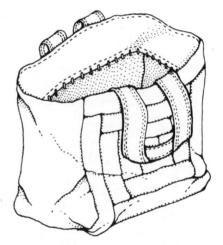

FIGURE 20:
Hand stitching the facing to the lining

SUGGESTIONS

I have several tote bags like this one. The first one I made has lasted two years of hard wear and has been washed oodles of times. I still get compliments on it!

The two sample blocks that you use for this project should be quilted. The quilting provides the major support of the bag. I've carried a gallon can of paint home in mine. You may want to use a waterproof lining.

The Translucent Appliqué in Block 8 will have to be backed with sturdy fabric first if you want to use it for this project. Or it also could be quilted to a heavy backing fabric.

The hen sitting on the nest in Block 14 would make a clever bag for the mother-to-be.

SIMPLIFICATIONS

Lining: The lining gives extra strength to the bag. It also protects the inside of the blocks and their seams from dirt and wear. Although it looks really nice, you can eliminate it to save time.

Make the bag eliminating any directions concerning the lining. Slipstitch the facing directly to the inside of the block and side pieces instead of the lining.

Eliminating one block: If you are giving these bags as Christmas presents as I have, you may want to take one other short cut.

For one of the quilted blocks, substitute a 15″ square of the bag fabric. It should be interfaced well so that it is equal to the quilted block in sturdiness. It is assembled in the same way. You then only need to make one quilted block; however, the bag will have obvious front and back sides.

CHAPTER FOUR

Block
4

Patchwork With Triangles

Some of the most lively patchwork designs that you see are made entirely with triangles. This technique merely takes Block 2: Patchwork With Squares one step further.

When a square is divided diagonally, two triangles are formed. You can make endless combinations by using different colored triangles. The combinations can be done at random or follow a carefully planned layout. The designs appear quite intricate when different colors are repeated in a set manner.

For this basic sample block, select three colors. Two of the colors should be similar in intensity. They can be contrasting colors, but they should look similar in brightness when they are placed side by side. The third color is a very dark or very light contrasting color that goes well with both of the other two colors. This is the predominant color in the design, and it is also used for the ends of the duffle bag in this chapter (if that's the project you're planning to make from the sample blocks). Choose fabrics that are sturdy, washable, and similar in weight.

SUPPLIES *(enough for four sample blocks)*

½ yard each of two different fabrics (**a** and **b**) and 1 yard of a third fabric (**c**).

> This is for the patchwork. The three should relate to each other well. They can be solids or prints. Identify them as colors **a, b,** and **c.** Color **c** is used twice as often as the other two so it should be your favorite of the three. Fabric **c** is also used for the ends of the duffle bag in this chapter. If you plan to do this project, get 1½ yards of fabric **c.**

Thread

> Select one color that blends with all three fabrics.

Cardboard 5″ x 5″ or larger

> One piece for making a template.

DIRECTIONS

Making the template:

This entire block of patchwork is made with one size template. Draw an exact 4½″ square on the piece of cardboard. Cut it out. Divide the square diagonally by drawing a line from one corner to the opposite corner. Do not cut yet. Select one of the triangles to be the template. Draw a line parallel to the diagonal line that is ½″ outside the selected triangle. This adds a ½″ seam allowance to the triangle template. Cut on this line. The seam allowances for the other two sides have already been included in the template.

Cutting:

Place the template on the wrong side of the fabric near the edge. The shorter straight sides of the template *must* match both the crosswise and lengthwise grains of the fabric. The diagonal side of the template will be a true bias.

Hold the template in place with one hand. Draw around it with the other. Use a pencil or marking pencil that is visible on the fabric. Repeat this procedure, positioning the triangles as close together as possible. You can fit many pieces together in a small area by interlocking them. This saves fabric if you are working with small scraps.

Cut the following number of triangles to make *one* sample block:

Color **a**   8 triangles
Color **b**   8 triangles
Color **c**   16 triangles

After you have drawn the correct number of triangles, cut them out on the lines you have drawn.

Assembling the triangles to form squares:

Place one triangle of color **a** on top of color **c**. The right sides should be together. Pin them together along the diagonal bias edge. Stitch a seam ½" from the raw edge (Figure 1A). Be careful not to stretch the bias edge when you are handling it. Avoid pulling the bias during sewing; it has a natural tendency to "grow" in length.

Press the diagonal seams open. Trim any excess seam allowance off if it extends beyond the edges of the square (Figure 1B).

Make eight squares by combining color **a** and color **c**. Make another eight squares by combining **b** and **c**. You can do this type of work in a sort of assembly line style. First pin all the seams together, then stitch them all, next press the seams open, and finally trim if necessary. You will have a total of sixteen squares.

Sewing the squares together:

Lay the squares out on the table with the right sides up. Use Figure 2 as a guide for positioning each square. Turn the squares and move them around until your squares are an exact copy of the plan in Figure 2.

Follow the steps given in Block 2: Patchwork With Squares to join these sixteen squares together. Match the seams and points carefully. Refer to Figure 2 to check the layout. The completed block measures 15" x 15"; this includes a ½" seam allowance on all sides.

This block is now ready to use. If you are making the Durable Duffle in the next part of this chapter, you need to make three more blocks that are identical to this one.

This block could be quilted if you plan a different project. Follow the quilting directions in Block 1.

Triangular patchwork is perfect for trying your hand at experimenting with color. Many different layouts can be made with just a few different colors. Use your own inventiveness to come up with your own design. Graph paper and colored pencils are the best way to experiment and plan color schemes for this patchwork. Assembling the triangles is always done in the same easy way, regardless of the color layout or size.

FIGURE 1

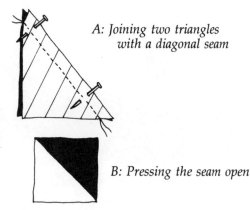

A: *Joining two triangles with a diagonal seam*

B: *Pressing the seam open*

FIGURE 2:
The completed sample block showing the arrangement of triangles

Project 4

A Durable Duffle

The project in this chapter uses *four* sample blocks that are not quilted. They are joined together and then quilted all at once by machine. This large square made from four blocks then becomes the body of the duffle bag. Brightly colored, quilted, and designed by you, it will surely be the center of attention in any ticket line.

SUPPLIES

four unquilted sample blocks

½ yard of solid color fabric

> This is for the circular end pieces. If you are using the Patchwork With Triangles, use color c.

1½ yards of muslin or lining fabric

1½ yards of quilt batting

two 14″ heavy duty zippers

> The zipper tape should blend with the colors in the four sample blocks. You can also use one 28″ zipper.

1½ yards of piping

> You may want to make your own piping in the bag fabric. If so, get ½ yard more fabric in color c. Also get 1½ yards of ¼″ cotton cord.

1¾ yards of 1½″ to 2½″ wide webbing

> For straps. Get a color that matches the blocks or the zipper.

Thread

> Use heavy duty thread.

4 D rings

> The same width as the webbing.

FIGURE 3:
*Four sample blocks joined together
and quilted in a giant zigzag diagram*

DIRECTIONS

Joining the four blocks:

Sew the four sample blocks together to form one large square for the body of the duffle bag. If you are using the Patchwork With Triangles, follow Figure 3 for the design layout.

To combine any other sample blocks, lay all four out together and select the best way to combine them yourself. Some sample blocks can be put together in any direction. Others form designs when they are joined so you should look at them together carefully before sewing.

Quilting the body of the bag:

Using the large square as a pattern, cut out a matching square of muslin and one of quilt batting.

Layer the batting between the muslin and the four joined sample blocks, right side up. Baste the three layers together so they are flat and even. This is a large square to quilt so make basting lines across the square at 6″ intervals. This holds the three layers together for easy quilting by hand or machine.

Quilt these three layers together as described in Block 1. The quilting lines should compliment or follow the design on the blocks. For Patchwork With Triangles, follow the patchwork by quilting with rows of giant zigzag lines across the square on top of the seams (Figure 3).

Attaching the zippers:

The two zippers are joined together so that the bag can be unzipped from the center. Pin the two tops of the zipper tapes together so that the zipper pulls face each other. Unzip the zippers. Sew the tops of the two tapes together by machine about ¼″ from the beginning of the zipper teeth. Press this seam open (Figure 4).

Overcast the raw edge on two opposite sides of the bag body. These sides will be sewn to the zipper. If you do not have a zigzag stitch for overcasting by machine, bind the edges with bias tape. This prevents threads and batting from unraveling and getting caught in the zipper.

Press under ½″ on both of the bound or overcast edges. Place one side on top of the zipper tape so that it is about ¼″ from teeth. Baste it in place through all layers. Machine stitch over your basting.

Bring the other bound edge around to the zipper tape

FIGURE 4:
*Attaching the two joined zippers
to the body of the duffle*

forming a cylinder with the bag body. Baste and sew this side in the same way as the first one. You will be working within the cylinder. Take care not to get the bag body caught in the stitching by accident. Tack the ends of the zipper tape together for easier working.

Attaching the D rings:

Cut two 3″ lengths of webbing. Encase the straight edge of each D ring by folding the piece of webbing in half through the ring. Baste the two raw edges of the webbing together (Figure 5A).

Center the raw edge of the webbing over one end of the zipper opening. Pin and baste it in place with the raw edges even (Figure 5B). Do the same thing at the other end of the zipper opening.

Quilting the end pieces:

Cut out two 12″ squares from the fabric for the ends of the duffle bag. Also cut two 12″ squares from the muslin and the quilt batting. Put the batting between the fabric and the muslin right side out. Make sure all the layers are smooth and flat. Baste them together along the outside raw edges. Baste an X through the center of the square securing all three layers together.

The quilting diagram for the end pieces is four concentric circles. Draw a 2″ circle on a piece of cardboard using a compass. Cut it out and place it in the exact center of the 12″ fabric square. You can locate the center easily by folding the square into quarters. Hold the circle in place and draw around it. This will become the center of the quilting diagram.

Hold your ruler so the 6″ mark is directly on the circle you have drawn. Make four marks outward from the center circle at 1″ intervals. Use a compass to draw concentric circles at these marks. The concentric circles can be drawn with a ruler if you prefer. Continue marking the 1″ intervals around the center circle. Be sure that the 6″ point of the ruler is always on the circle (Figure 6). When you have moved the ruler entirely around the center circle, you will have drawn four circles that are equally spaced 1″ apart around the center circle.

Hand or machine quilt through all three layers on the inner *four* circles that you have drawn. Refer to Block 1 for quilting directions.

After the quilting is completed, cut it out on the fifth outer circle. Baste all the layers together about ½″ from the raw edges (Figure 7).

A: A D ring carrier made from webbing

B: Positioning the D rings on the body of the duffle

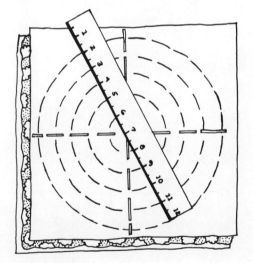

FIGURE 6:
Drawing the quilting diagram of concentric circles on the end pieces of the duffle

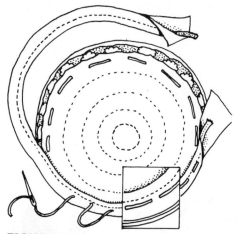

FIGURE 7:
*Opening the ends of the piping.
Basting the piping to
the quilted end pieces*

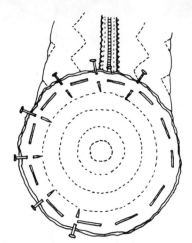

FIGURE 8:
*Sewing the end pieces to the
body of the duffle*

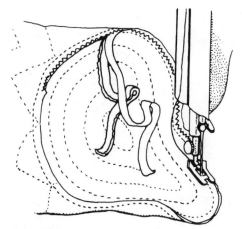

FIGURE 9:
*Overcasting and trimming the
seam allowance of the end pieces*

Applying the piping to the end pieces:

You can buy piping that is already made up, or you can make it yourself from the bag fabric. Piping that you make in matching fabric looks a lot better than the piping available in stores.

The piping is applied in the same manner as described in Project 2: A Pushover of a Pillow. Cut two pieces of piping that measure 30″ long. Leave open, or remove the stitches at all four ends, for about 2″ (Figure 7). This allows you to join the two ends of piping easily.

On the right side, match the raw edges of the piping to the raw edges of the quilted circular end piece. Pin and baste in place around the entire circle (Figure 7). Join the ends of the piping with a seam as described in Project 2, Figure 8. Machine stitch around piping.

Attaching the end pieces to the bag body:

Turn the bag body inside out. Begin at the zipper, and make a mark every 7″ along both ends of the bag body. This will divide the edge into fourths. Check your marks by folding the ends into fourths. The zipper is the top. The marks 7″ from the zipper are the side points. The remaining mark is the bottom.

Fold the quilted end pieces into fourths. Make marks on the wrong side at each crease.

Position the end piece on the bag body so that the right side is inside. Put one of the marks at the zipper. Match the three other marks to the marks on the bag body. Pin the entire end piece in place, easing in the slight fullness in between the marks. Baste the end piece to the bag body (Figure 8). Your stitches should be on top of the basting stitches that hold the piping in place. Open the zipper partially, and repeat this on the other end.

Sew the end pieces in by machine using a zipper foot. Your stitches should be on top of the basting stitches. Be careful not to catch another part of the bag with this stitching. Overcast this seam next to your stitching, and trim the excess fabric away (Figure 9). Turn the bag right side out.

Making a shoulder strap:

Cut the webbing piece in half. Fold back 3″ of one end of one of the pieces. Insert two D rings onto the webbing. Turn under ¼″ on the raw edge. Stitch a box with an X through it on the webbing securing the two layers together (Figure 10) and enclosing the D rings.

Hem one end of the other piece of webbing by turning the raw edge under ¼" twice. Stitch across the end to hold the hem in place.

Turn under ¼" on the remaining raw ends of the two pieces. Fold back 3" on both ends. Insert them into the D rings on the duffle bag. Stitch on each side as shown in Figure 11. This box of stitching with an X in the center is a very strong and durable way to attach straps.

SUGGESTIONS

This duffle bag can do a lot more than hold everything you need for a weekend vacation. Leave off the D rings and the handle to use it as a giant bolster pillow. Inside you can store an extra blanket or two.

The instructions are given using four sample blocks; however, you can use the same basic construction using only two blocks for a roomy shoulder bag. Or leave the straps off this small version, stuff it tightly with a rolled-up blanket for a hassock.

Make a few bags in the smaller version to use as brightly colored, inconspicuous storage drums. Masquerading as pillows, they're perfect for hiding the mounds of yarn, fabrics, and leftover batting in your sewing area.

If all this sounds absurd, and all you really want is a duffle bag, it needn't be exactly like the pictured version. Try experimenting with different kinds of straps. Use a buckle instead of D rings. Try attaching a strap to one end piece so it can be carried vertically. Or both ends so two people can carry it together. You might add a lining with some zippered pockets inside.

SIMPLIFICATIONS

Piping: Although the piping gives stability to the bag, it could be eliminated altogether. Attach the end pieces to the bag just as shown, merely eliminating the part about piping.

Shoulder strap: The D rings on the shoulder strap make it adjustable and replaceable. If you like, you can use one continuous piece of webbing for a shoulder strap. Eliminate any steps that involve D rings.

Cut one piece of webbing 40" long. Test this length for comfortable carrying. Usually, the taller the person, the longer the strap. Attach the strap at both ends of the zipper. Center the raw edge of the webbing over the zipper. The raw edge should be even with the raw edge of the bag body. Make sure the strap is not twisted before you sew it in the seams!

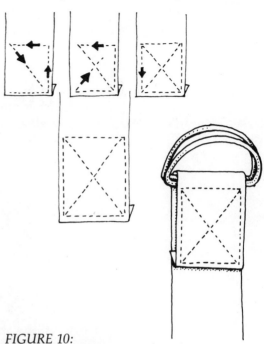

FIGURE 10:
*The steps involved
in making a square of stitching
with an X in the center*

FIGURE 11:
*The completed duffle showing the
two-piece shoulder strap*

CHAPTER FIVE

Block 5 # Patchwork With Strips

Patchwork with strips has the distinction of being the fastest and the easiest patchwork technique. This is really a blessing when you want good results in a hurry. The design doesn't suffer because of the speediness either. This technique, like almost all patchwork, can be done well using scraps or fabrics chosen at random. However, the best designs are deliberately planned with colors that repeat over and over. There are also several ways to make larger complicated-looking designs by sewing groups of four blocks together.

Whatever you plan to make, this technique provides you with a way to assemble large areas with a minimum of seaming. It's perfect for a bedspread or quilt.

For this sample block, select three different fabrics, one light shade, one medium shade, and one dark one. They can be printed or solid fabrics, but they all should go together well because they are assembled next to each other.

The stitching goes quickly. Long, narrow strips of the three fabrics are sewn together. This strip of the three colors combined is then cut at measured intervals, forming squares. Four squares are then assembled to form one sample block. If you are doing a project that requires hundreds of blocks, this technique is a real time-saver.

SUPPLIES: *(enough for one sample block)*

⅛ yard each of three different color fabrics
> One of the fabrics should be a light color, one a medium color, and the third should be dark. They need not be similar in weight.

½ yard of muslin
½ yard of quilt batting
Thread
> Pick out one color that blends with all three fabrics. Black works well with color mixtures like this. It will be used for seams and for quilting.

DIRECTIONS

Cutting:

Be sure to straighten your fabrics before you begin cutting. Strips are cut along the crossgrain of the fabric so you need to begin with an absolutely straight edge.

Draw a line across the entire width of one of the fabrics that is 3⅜″ from the straightened edge. It will be parallel to the cut edge. Cut on this line. Repeat this on the other two fabrics. You will need one strip in each fabric to make one sample block.

Making the patchwork squares:

Pin the three strips of fabric together, placing the dark color in the center. Use a ½″ seam allowance. Sew these two long seams that join the three strips together by machine. Press the seams open. The center strip will be narrower because the seam allowances on both sides have been used up (Figure 1). The combined strip should be 8″ wide.

Square off one end of the strip so that it is perfectly straight. Measure 8″ from this end along the raw edge on both sides of the strip. Make a mark on both raw edges at the 8″ points. Connect these marks with a line. Cut on this line. Continue cutting 8″ squares from the rest of the strip (Figure 1).

You need four 8″ patchwork squares to complete one sample block. Make as many patchwork squares as you need at one time.

Four 8″ squares are joined to make each sample block. Position all the light color strips so they intersect at the center of the block. This forms a pinwheel design in the center of the block.

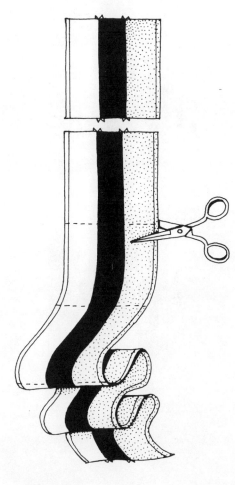

FIGURE 1:
Joining three long strips of fabric and cutting patchwork squares from it

FIGURE 2

A: Pinwheel layout

B: Ladder or zigzag layout

C: Checkerboard layout

Refer to Block 2, Figures 3 and 4, for instructions on joining squares. Use a ½" seam allowance. Press all the seams open.

Quilting the sample block:

Cut a 15" square of muslin and quilt batting. Place the batting between the muslin and the patchwork. Prepare the block for quilting by basting it as described in Block 1, Figures 1 and 2.

The quilting diagram for this block is composed of concentric triangles. (They all have the same center.) Use your clear ruler to draw the diagram lightly on the block.

Draw an X through the center of the block. This divides the block into four triangles. Draw two more triangles inside each of the four triangles. The space between each triangle is 1". The base line of the first triangle you draw should be 1" from the *seamline* along the raw edge of the block. That is 1½" from the raw edge. Use a clear ruler to draw the lines. You can quickly align the clear ruler along one line and draw the entire second line 1" away from it.

Quilt the entire block on the quilting diagram you have drawn. Refer to Block 1 for the specific steps of quilting.

This block is now ready to use for a project. The Blockbuster of a Backpack in the next part of this chapter is a useful project that uses only one quilted block.

This type of patchwork is excellent for very large projects as well. It sews up very quickly and can be combined in a number of ways (Figure 2). Try it for a tablecloth or quilt or a large wall hanging.

A Blockbuster of a Backpack

Project 5

The project in this chapter uses *one* sample block that has been quilted. The block is used for the closing flap on the backpack. Use lightweight canvas or heavy fabric in a color that matches the sample block to make the body of the bag. Bright or light reflective fabrics are a good idea for the flap of the bag. If you use the backpack while riding your bicycle, you'll be visible for blocks!

SUPPLIES

One quilted sample block

1¼ yards of heavy fabric

> This will be used for the body of the backpack and the ties. Pick out something heavy that will wear well. It should go with the colors in the sample block.

1 yard of lining fabric in a dark color

1¼ yards of 1½" or 2" wide webbing

> For the straps. If you can't find a good color match, you can make your own straps from the backpack fabric. Get ¼ yard extra fabric.

4 D rings

> The same width as the webbing.

Thread

> Use heavy duty thread.

DIRECTIONS

Cutting:

The entire bag, except for the flap, is made from the heavy fabric. The flap is lined with the fabric. Plot out the dimensions of the pieces you'll need, and draw them right on your fabric before cutting. This prevents you from wasting fabric and makes sure that you fit all the pieces in before you cut. Draw and cut them out in the order they are given. The straight edges of the pieces should be on the crosswise or lengthwise grain of the fabric.

> one 41" x 4½" (facing for the top edge of the bag)
> three 15" x 15" (front, back, and flap lining)
> three 7" x 15" (bottom and two sides)
> four 2" x 12" (four tie ends)

Cut from the lining fabric:

> two 15" x 15" (front and back)
> three 7" x 15" (bottom and two sides)

Making the tie ends:

Follow the instructions given in Project 1, Figures 13 and 14, for making the ties. Turn under ½" on only *one* end of each tie. The other end will be left raw. Topstitch the ties so that they are extra strong and durable.

Decide what side of the sample block should be the

FIGURE 3:
Basting the ties to the sample block and the front of the bag

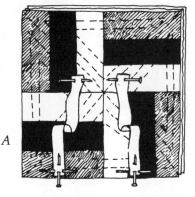

A

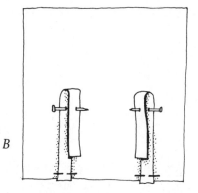

B

top. Baste two of the ties to the block 3½″ in from the sides. The raw edges of the ties should be even with the raw edges of the block. Pin the loose ends of the ties to the center of the block so they don't get caught in any seams (Figure 3A).

Baste the other two ties to one of the 15″ fabric squares. This will be the front of the bag. They also should be 3½″ in from the sides and raw edges even. Pin the loose ends (Figure 3B).

The bag straps:

This project can be made as a backpack or a shoulder bag. If you want to make the backpack, the straps are inserted onto the back of the backpack before you put it together. The straps can be adjusted with the D rings at the bottom of the backpack. These are also basted in place before assembling.

Cut two 3″ pieces of webbing. Prepare the D ring holders as shown in Project 4, Figure 5. Put *two* D rings on each holder. Baste them to one edge of one of the 15″ squares. They should be 3½″ in from the sides of the square (Figure 4).

Cut the remaining webbing in half. Hem one end of each piece. Baste the raw edges of the webbing to the back square opposite the D rings. They should be 3½″ in from the sides, also (Figure 4).

If you want to make your own straps from matching fabric, cut out one piece that measures 38″ x 4½″. See Project 3, Figure 15, for how to make the pieces for the straps. Attach them as shown in Figure 4.

Assembling the body of the backpack:

Sew the body of the bag together as shown in Project 3, Figures 10, 11, and 12. Plain fabric squares with the ties and straps basted on them make the front and back of the backpack rather than the quilted sample blocks shown in the illustrations.

Use the square with the ties as the front of the backpack. The ties should be sewn into the seam at the *bottom* of the front. The D rings are at the *bottom* of the back. The straps are opposite the D rings on the back piece so they will be at the top of the backpack.

The lining:

Put the lining together in the same way that you did the backpack body. Insert it into the backpack. The wrong sides of the backpack and the lining should be

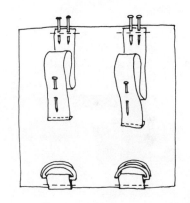

FIGURE 4:
Basting the straps and the D rings in place to the back piece

together as shown in Project 3, Figure 13. Evenly match and baste the top raw edges together as in Project 3, Figure 14.

Making the flap:

Place the one remaining 15″ fabric square on top of the sample block with the right sides together. Pin and baste them together, leaving the *top* side of the block open. Sew the two sides and the bottom of the flap. The ties will be secured at the same time.

Trim and grade the raw edges and corners as done in Project 1, Figure 5. Turn the flap right side out. Press it flat. Baste the top side closed with the raw edges together.

Attaching the flap to the backpack:

Match the raw edges of the flap and the back side of the backpack. The *right* side of the sample block should be against the outside of the backpack, on top of the straps and the D rings. Baste the flap in this position ½″ from the raw edges through all thicknesses (Figure 5).

Making the facing:

Follow the instructions in Project 3, Figures 17, 18, 19, and 20, to construct and attach the facing to the backpack. It will have straps and ties rather than handles like the bag in the illustrations. See Figures 6A and 6B for a view of the completed backpack.

Shoulder bag version:

To make this version, assemble the backpack as it is illustrated, eliminating the insertion of straps and D rings.

The shoulder strap is approximately 30″ long. Test this length to be sure it is comfortable for you. Cut a piece of webbing or make your own matching fabric strap in the correct length. Hem both ends of the strap.

Center the ends of the straps on the sides of the backpack 5″ down from the top edge (Figure 7). Sew the ends in place as demonstrated in Project 4, Figure 10.

SUGGESTIONS

If you aren't the backpack type, make the shoulder bag version. This project packs a lunch and a canteen just as easily as it does a stack of diapers and a baby bottle.

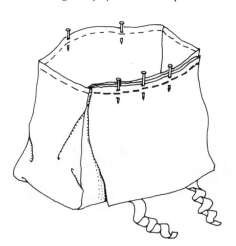

FIGURE 5:
Attaching the flap to the backpack

FIGURE 6

A: The backpack tied closed

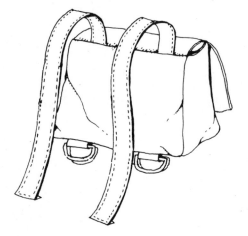

B: The straps for carrying

Make the decorative flap of the backpack out of light reflective fabrics for a bicycle rider. It would be a terrific safety idea that couldn't be missed on the road. If you plan to take it camping, quilt the flap with extra-thick batting and roll it up for a perfect pillow.

Another suggestion from an old backpacker is to quilt the *back* piece of the backpack. Speaking from painful experience, this would be a great added comfort, protecting your back from the sharp pokes it would otherwise get from things like camera accessories, flashlights, etcetera. Fussing with wrapping extra socks around can openers and telephoto lenses can be a lot of extra work and still not be a comfy solution.

Adapt two backpacks saddlebag style for a large dog as shown in the beginning of the instructions. They are soft and light. Make straps to custom fit the dog, and get him to stand still long enough for a fitting.

SIMPLIFICATIONS

Lining: If the fabric you're using is very heavy, you can eliminate the lining. Be sure to overcast all the inside seams. Sew the facing down right to the sides of the backpack.

Straps: The D rings make the backpack adjustable. The straps could be sewn directly into the bottom seam of the backpack. Use the same spacing. Be sure to measure the length of the straps on yourself and test them for comfort.

Before you decide you can do without the D rings, consider: Do you always wear the same clothes when you backpack? If you're likely to be wearing a bulky sweater or down jacket one time and a T-shirt another time, you may want the D rings for their variable strap adjustments in order to be comfortable no matter what you're wearing. Also, if a friend offers to carry your backpack, you will certainly want to be able to adjust it to a different size.

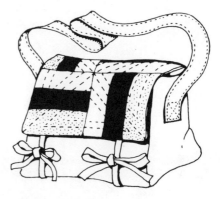

FIGURE 7:
The shoulder bag version

CHAPTER SIX

Block 6

Patchwork Without a Pattern

This technique of patchwork is often erroneously called "crazy quilting." But it is not what its name *implies*—neither crazy or quilted. I am told the term "crazy" was originally given to it because the design resembled cracked or crazed ice. That may very well be true; however, as you may remember from reading the instructions and definitions for quilting given in Block 1, this technique is most certainly *not* quilting.

Patchwork without a pattern is the best technique for using up every bit of your fabric scraps, no matter what shape, color, or size they are. This technique works well with all kinds of fabrics. Often, the stranger the combination, the more vibrant the patchwork.

This is a plan-as-you-patch pattern. Starting in one corner of a square of muslin, you cover it with patches that you cut out as you work. If you need a tiny, sort-of-triangular piece, you select one from your scrap pile and trim it to fit.

The patches are held in place by hand embroidery or machine stitches. The raw edges of each are turned under, as in appliqué, to prevent unraveling. When the edge of one piece is overlapped by another, you need only turn under the edge of the top piece.

For this sample block, the edges of the patches are covered with rickrack. It is not necessary to turn under any raw edges. The patches are held in place by a fabric fuser. The patches overlap slightly, and the rickrack is applied by machine.

Each completed block has an individual character that would be difficult to duplicate exactly. No two blocks will look the same even if you are using the same fabrics. When several blocks are joined together, the seamed edges form an intriguing design regardless of how you combine them.

SUPPLIES *(enough for one sample block)*

Fabrics

Assemble your favorite pieces from the scrap bag. You will need an assortment of about fifteen different fabrics. Any size or shape scraps will do.

1 yard of fabric fuser

This is used to secure small pieces to the backing square.

½ yard of muslin

If your scraps are lace or sheer fabrics, the backing fabric should be white or a solid color that blends with the sheer scraps. It will show through the scrap fabrics.

2 yards of rickrack

Select one color, or two or three different colors. The rickrack should accent your fabric scraps. Black or white is a good choice for most fabrics if you only want one color.

Thread

It should match the rickrack. If you are using many colors of rickrack, pick one color of thread that will go well with all the colors.

DIRECTIONS

Cutting:

Cut a 15″ square from the muslin. The pieces for this patchwork are cut as you work. Cut a circle 6″ or 8″ in diameter from one of the fabrics. Fold the circle into quarters. Cut on the fold lines. Cut three more circles of approximately the same size from three other fabrics. Fold and cut them in the same way. The circles need not be the same size.

The patchwork layout:

Place one of the pie-slice-shaped pieces on the fabric fuser. Cut the fuser to the exact same size as the fabric piece. Pin or baste them together. Repeat this with three more of the one-quarter circle pieces. Each one should be from a different fabric.

Fit each piece (backed with the fabric fuser) into a corner of the backing square. The right side of the fabric should be up. Make sure that none of the fabric fuser extends beyond the edge of the fabric. This would come in direct contact with your iron and melt onto the iron.

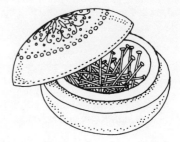

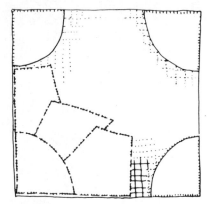

FIGURE 1:
Positioning the four corner pieces, and starting to fill in the center of the block

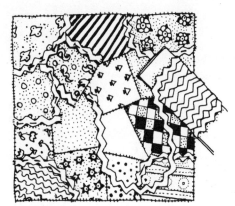

FIGURE 2:
Covering the raw edges of the patches with rickrack

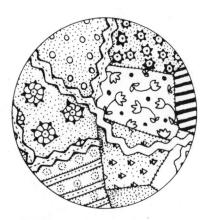

FIGURE 3:
A detail of the rickrack application showing the machine stitching and overlapping of the rickrack ends

Fuse the pieces in place with your iron. Use a piece of scrap muslin as a press cloth over the block to protect your iron from any stray pieces of fuser. The fuser secures each piece in place and seals the raw edges so they don't fray.

Pieces are cut from your scraps to fill in the spaces between the four corners. Each patch is backed with fuser and sealed into place individually.

The patches can be cut any way you like. You need not follow a grainline. The edges can overlap slightly. Do not cut all the pieces at once. Cut one or two at a time and then fuse them to the backing square. The edges of these pieces give you the outline for the next piece (Figure 1).

Examine the edges where the next piece will go, and cut a piece to fit. Test it. When it is the correct shape to correspond with the patchwork already in place, cut the fuser to fit, and secure it in position. Continue cutting and fusing patches in this way until the entire block is covered.

Applying the rickrack to the raw edges:

The raw edges of each patch are to be concealed with rickrack. Use all one color or any arrangement of different colors that you like.

Begin at the straight edges of the block. Pin and baste the rickrack in place over the edges of the patchwork (Figure 2). Change colors as often as you like.

Tuck under the ends of the rickrack when you change colors. Ends can also be hidden under each other at intersections (Figure 3).

When all the patchwork edges are covered with rickrack, machine stitch it in place. One row of machine stitching is made through the center of the rickrack. If it is necessary to stop stitching at an intersection, make a few reverse stitches to secure the thread ends.

A zigzag stitch or a machine embroidery stitch could also be used in the center of the rickrack. Trimmings other than rickrack would work well. They should be no wider than ½" and very flat.

The block is ready to use for a project. If the project calls for a quilted block, back it with batting and backing fabric. Tuft this block rather than quilting it. Place the tufts at the rickrack intersections.

If you plan to make A Timeless Tablecloth in part two of this chapter, you will need sixteen sample blocks.

AN ACE OF AN APRON
One block of "Basic Quilting" is used for
the bib of each apron. The blocks are made
by hand quilting cotton scarves, and
the skirt sections are of matching fabric.

A PUSHOVER OF A PILLOW
One "Patchwork With Squares" block is used for the quilted pillow.
The matching quilt, made with 16 blocks, has a 4" bias ruffle border
and measures 64" square.

A TAG-ALONG TOTE
Two "Patchwork With Rectangles" blocks are used for each bag, forming the
front and the back. The handles and sides of the totes are made
with brightly colored heavy fabric.

A DURABLE DUFFLE
Four "Patchwork With Triangles" blocks are joined and quilted to form the body of each duffle bag. The end pieces are quilted and edged with piping.

A BLOCKBUSTER OF A BACKPACK
One "Patchwork With Strips" block is used for the flap of each backpack. They are machine quilted. The straps of two backpacks are joined to make a bicycle saddlebag.

A TIMELESS TABLECLOTH
Sixteen "Patchwork Without a Pattern"
blocks are joined to make the tablecloth.
It has a 4" white bias ruffle
and measures 64" square.

A CLEVER CLUTCH
One "Appliqué With Trims" block is used
to make the clutch purse, which is lined
with white satin. The satin ties are
edge-stitched in place by machine.

CREATIVE CAFÉ CURTAINS
Four "Translucent Appliqué" blocks are used
to make these panels. The colored organdy
leaves are hand appliquéd in a
circular design to white organdy.

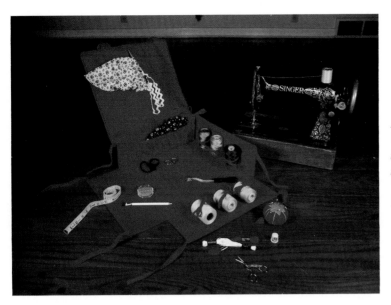

A SUPER SEWING BOX
One "Cut-away Appliqué" block is used for
the lid of the sewing box. Inside are
two large convenient pockets.
The box itself is made of broadcloth,
lined with heavy cardboard supports.

A PERKY PICNIC PACK
One "Lacy Appliqué" block forms the center of the pack. It is machine appliqued
and quilted in black thread. Red broadcloth and gingham
make up the rest of the pack.

A BEACH BLANKET BUNDLE
One "Corded Quilting" block is used as a pillow/towel pocket. Blue and yellow terry cloth is used for the sections of the bundle, with pockets of matching broadcloth.

A TRAVELING TREASURE CASE
One "Stuffed Quilting" block made from lavender velour is used for the outside of the case. The inside is matching faille fabric.

A PERFECT PLACEMAT
One "Mock Smocking" block is used to make each placemat. The material is yellow broadcloth, with red stitching.

A QUESTIONING QUILT
Twelve different "Picture Appliqué" blocks are used for the broadcloth quilt.
The appliqué and outlines are satin stitched
by machine in black thread. The eyes are all
satin stitched by hand. The borders are machine quilted.

Project 6 A Timeless Tablecloth

The project in this chapter is a tablecloth, and it uses *sixteen* sample blocks. The completed tablecloth measures 60″ square. The blocks can be quilted or unquilted. They are joined together, and the edges of the tablecloth are bound with a fabric border. This basic project is very versatile. It can double as a lap robe or a wall hanging. Fold it diagonally and add fringe for a large shawl, or use it flat as a crib blanket for a new baby.

SUPPLIES

Sixteen sample blocks
> They can be quilted with a thin layer of fleece or used unquilted.

1¾ yards of solid color fabric
> This is for the border of the tablecloth. It should accent the colors in the sample blocks that you are using. Use light or medium weight fabric.

Thread
> To match the solid fabric.

DIRECTIONS

Joining the sample blocks:

Lay all the sample blocks out together. Move them around until you find the arrangement that you like best. Assemble them as shown in Block 2, Figures 3 and 4. Join them with a ½" seam allowance and press the seams open. Trim the seam allowances diagonally where they overlap.

This tablecloth is unlined. Overcast the seams on the wrong side with a zigzag stitch so they don't fray.

Making the border:

Cut four strips that each measure 5" wide from the solid fabric. Cut these strips on the lengthwise grain of the fabric, parallel to the selvage. Each strip will be 1¾ yards long.

Press under ½" on both long edges of each strip. Fold the strip in half lengthwise and match the pressed under edges. Press a lengthwise crease down the center of each strip. The finished width of the border strip is 2".

Find the halfway point of each piece by folding it in half and creasing it crosswise. Open out one of the ½" seam allowances of one strip. Match this middle point with the center seam on one side of the tablecloth. Pin the strip to the edge of the tablecloth with the right sides together. Match the raw edges. Pin along the crease line in the strip ½" from the edge of the tablecloth.

Sew this seam by machine beginning and ending ½" from the edge of the tablecloth corner (Figure 4). Backtrack, or tie the ends of your threads at this point.

Working flat, fold the strip away from the tablecloth so that it makes a 45° angle fold at the point where the stitching stops (Figure 5).

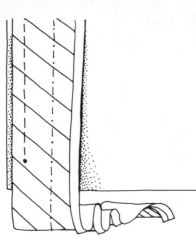

FIGURE 4:
Stitching the border to within ½" of the edge of the tablecloth corner

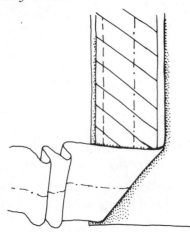

FIGURE 5:
Folding the border strip diagonally outward

Match the end of a second strip with the first one. Place the right sides together over the 45° angle fold. Measure 4½" out horizontally from the middle crease line of the first strip (the one underneath). This measurement is twice the width of the finished border plus a ½" seam allowance. Cut off both strips at this point. Seam the two strips together ½" from this cut end (Figure 6).

Match the raw edges of the two strips along the lower edge. The raw edge of the second strip (the one on top) will match the edge of the tablecloth. Pin these edges together and machine stitch them using a ½" seam allowance (Figure 6). Attach the second strip to the edge of the tablecloth stopping ½" from the next corner.

Open out the mitered corner. Make sure the corner is square with an L square. Put a pin on the right side of the strip, securing the diagonal fold flat in place (Figure 7). Slipstitch this fold closed up to the corner where the seam emerges.

Turn the corner over. Trim off the fabric corner with the seam allowances intersecting on it about ¼" from the slipstitches (Figure 8).

Press the seam allowances toward the strip. Neatly tuck the seam into the pointed corner of the strip so

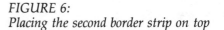

FIGURE 6:
Placing the second border strip on top

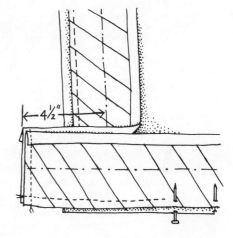

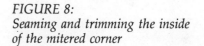

FIGURE 7:
Mitering the right side of the corner

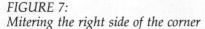

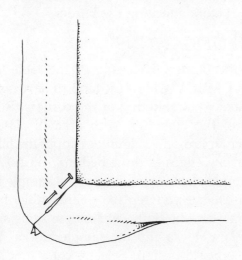

FIGURE 8:
Seaming and trimming the inside
of the mitered corner

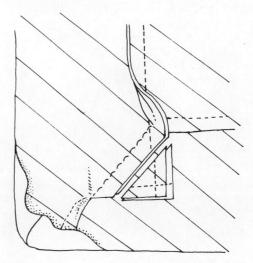

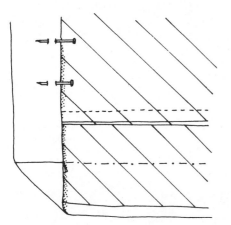

FIGURE 9:
*Folding the border in place
on the wrong side of the tablecloth
along one edge*

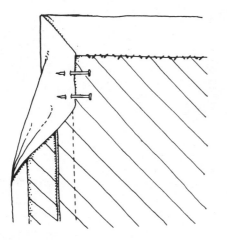

FIGURE 10:
*Completing the mitered corner
on the wrong side of the tablecloth,
and stitching the edges in place*

everything inside lies flat. Fold the first strip in half along the middle crease. Pin it in place where the strip meets the wrong side of the tablecloth (Figure 9).

Fold the corner in along the seam of the two strips. The opposite edge of the strip will meet the tablecloth at the same time. Pin the corner 45° angle fold in place. Slipstitch the corner closed. Slipstitch the edge of the strip to the tablecloth (Figure 10). Repeat this process on each corner of the tablecloth.

SUGGESTIONS

This tablecloth is one of the easiest projects to make. It uses sixteen sample blocks so most of your time will be spent making the blocks.

If you don't need a 60″ tablecloth, or if you would like to use it as a shawl, make it from only four sample blocks. This will make a finished square that measures 32″ x 32″.

Either tablecloth can be made slightly larger or smaller by varying the width of the border. It could be as narrow as 1″ or as wide as 6″. Be sure to change the cutting and mitering measurements if you change this width of the border. Get 2 yards of fabric for the strips if you enlarge the border.

The tablecloth could be lined if you like. Use a contrasting solid color that goes well with the border fabric. This will make the tablecloth reversible so it will get twice the use. Simply back the combined blocks with fabric before attaching the border.

SIMPLIFICATIONS

Fabric border: The edge of the tablecloth could be bound with 1″ wide bias tape to save time. This also eliminates the mitering of the corners. Round the corners of the tablecloth with a small plate in the way shown in Project 7, Figure 6. Apply the bias tape to the outer raw edges as described in Project 7, Figure 8.

Sample blocks: One half of the sample blocks can be eliminated if you replace them with a block of plain fabric. The tablecloth remains the same size. Alternate the plain blocks and the sample blocks. This creates a checkerboard design. Select a color that goes with the sample blocks. Cut eight 15″ squares and make only eight sample blocks.

CHAPTER SEVEN

Block 7 · Appliqué With Trims

Appliqué is a decorative sewing technique that is done by stitching small cut-out pieces to a larger background. The small pieces are sewn to the background by hand or machine to form a design or picture. When necessary the edges of the appliquéd pieces are turned under to prevent fraying. The hand stitch that is generally used is called the slipstitch. The machine stitch can be straight or a form of machine embroidery such as the zigzag or satin stitch.

This style of appliqué is done with different widths of ribbons and trimmings that can be found in packages or bought by the yard. It is a good way to use up even the wildest combinations of leftover lace, tapes, and braids. Sometimes you can buy a large bag of assorted trims very cheaply. There are hundreds of types of ribbons, metallic braids, laces, satins, velvets, and endless tapes with woven designs. Select trims and colors for the look you want: fancy, plain, sporty, or even match an outfit that has the same trim.

This technique could also be done with an assortment of scrap fabrics. You can put even the smallest scraps to good use! They are cut into strips of varying widths and sewn to a muslin backing. A combination of fabric and trimmings is okay if you like. Instructions are given for working with fabrics or ribbon.

This block is made up of four squares. If the trims you select have cut-out areas like lace, select a bright colored solid fabric for the background squares. When you appliqué the lace trim, the color will show through.

Rows of trims are appliquéd to each square diagonally. Trims have finished or woven edges. This eliminates the job of turning under raw edges. Sew the trims to the squares using fancy machine stitches if you have them on your machine. If not, you can use bright contrasting thread and stitch by hand or machine.

SUPPLIES *(enough for one sample block)*

Ribbons and trims

Collect about ten or twelve different ones. You need about 1 yard of each. To make this block with fabric, choose the same number of different fabrics.

½ yard muslin

Thread

Get any color that blends with the fabrics or trims you have picked out.

DIRECTIONS

Cutting:

Cut four perfect 8″ squares from the muslin. If you are using scrap fabrics rather than ribbons, cut the scrap fabric into strips. These strips can vary in width from 1″ to 3″. They all should be cut on the straight grain of the fabric. Each one should be 11½″ long to cross the 8″ square diagonally.

Making the appliquéd squares with fabric:

Fold each 8″ square diagonally. Press a crease across the squares. Open one of the squares out on a flat surface (Figure 1A).

Put all your fabric strips out on the table. Move them

FIGURE 1:
Creasing the muslin square, and applying the first strip of fabric

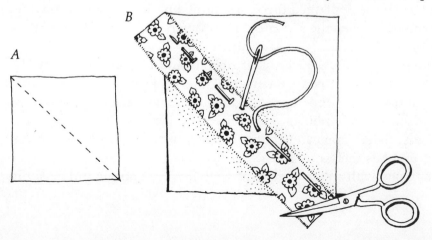

around next to each other until you find the order you like best.

Take the center strip and place it on the muslin square so that the raw edge is aligned with the diagonal crease. Pin and baste the strip in place ¼" away from the crease. Trim off the excess fabric that extends beyond the muslin (Figure 1B). Save any long portions of the strips that you cut off, to use later.

Working out from the center, place the second strip on top of the first one with the right sides together. Match the raw edges at the creaseline. Pin the second strip in place and baste it using a ¼" seam allowance. Machine stitch over the basting (Figure 2). Press the second strip over so that the seam is covered and the right side is up. Trim off the extra fabric (Figure 3). Baste the remaining raw edge flat in place.

Continue working in the same way until one half of the square is covered with strips. The seams should all be straight and parallel to each other (Figure 4). Work in the same way on the other side of the center strip until the entire square is covered.

One sample block is made up of four 8" squares. Make three more squares. They can be identical to the first one, or each one can have a different arrangement of strips.

Making the appliquéd squares with ribbon or trim:

The four 8" squares are covered with ribbon, lace, or trimmings in almost the same way as with fabric. The only difference is that the trims have woven edges. They do not need to be seamed and turned over as with the fabric strips. They are easier to use. Plan the layout before starting.

Fold the muslin squares diagonally and crease them. Align the woven edge of the center trim with the creaseline. The right side is up. Place the next trim so that it butts up against the first one. Baste all the trims in place and trim the excess ends away. There should not be any space between trims. Cover all four squares with trim.

Do all the stitching at one time. Make a row of straight stitching very close to the two woven edges of each trim. If your machine does zigzag or embroidery stitches, center one row of stitching over the two woven edges. This secures both pieces of trim at one time. It also adds a decorative touch. Try using several different stitches and changing the thread color.

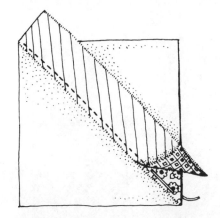

FIGURE 2:
Placing the second strip on top of the first one with the right sides together

FIGURE 3:
Pressing the second strip to the right side

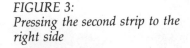

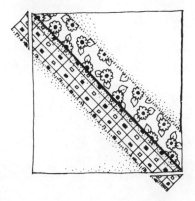

FIGURE 4:
Covering the square with fabric strips

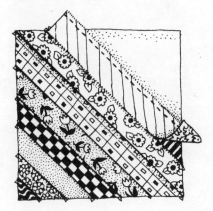

FIGURE 5:
Four squares joined to make one sample block

Joining the squares:

Sew the four squares together. Use a ½" seam allowance. The seams should intersect at the center of the block (Figure 5). Press the seams open and trim the intersection diagonally. If all four squares are identical, the strips will match at the seams. They need not match exactly to look good!

This block is ready to use for A Clever Clutch in the second part of this chapter. It does not need to be quilted.

If you are using this block for a project that requires a quilted block, add a layer of batting and muslin. This design would look great quilted or tufted. This block, like many of the other sample blocks, looks very good when many blocks are sewn together. Diamond shapes are formed at the intersections of each block. It can also be done well in any size, smaller or larger than the sample block.

Corduroy or velvet scraps would make an interesting, textured pattern. Try alternating laces and satin ribbons appliquéd to a contrasting background fabric. Experiment with all your leftovers and challenge yourself to combine them creatively.

Project 7

A Clever Clutch

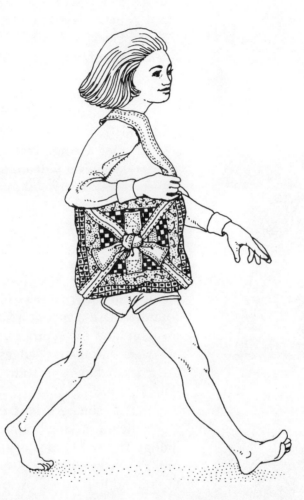

The project in this chapter uses *one* sample block that can be quilted or unquilted. The block is bound on all edges and folded to make a neat clutch purse. You attach a shoulder strap, if you like, and tie ends for a closure. Depending on your selection of trims, this purse will easily add a spark to an evening gown or an accent to jeans and a khaki shirt.

SUPPLIES

One sample block
> It can be quilted or unquilted.

½ yard interfacing
> Use medium or lightweight interfacing.

½ yard lining
> Select a lining fabric in a color that accents the sample block.

2 yards of 1″ wide bias tape
> Pick a color that goes well with the sample block.

1½ yards of 1½″ or 2″ wide grosgrain ribbon or webbing
> This is for the tie and shoulder strap. It can also be made from fabric if you like.

Thread
> Get a color that matches the bias tape and whatever you are using for the shoulder strap.

DIRECTIONS

Cutting:

The four outer corners of the sample block must be rounded. Use a medium-sized tumbler as a template. Position it on each corner so that the edges of the glass are even with the raw edges of the block. Draw around the glass making a smooth, rounded corner. Cut on the line (Figure 6).

Cut a 15″ square from the lining and the interfacing. Layer the interfacing between the sample block and the lining. The right sides of the lining and the block are out. Pin them together. Round the corners of the interfacing and lining to correspond to the sample block.

Binding the edges of the clutch with bias tape:

Baste the sample block, interfacing, and lining squares together ½″ from the raw edges. Bias tape 1″ wide is applied around the outer raw edges (Figure 7). There are two ways to apply bias tape. If you are working with an unquilted sample block, use the one-step method. If your block is quilted or made of very thick fabric, use the two-step technique.

The *one-step application* is good for binding flat or thin edges. Press the tape in half lengthwise. One of the long

FIGURE 6:
Using a glass to round the corners of the sample block

FIGURE 7:
Applying bias tape to the edge of the sample block

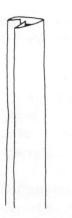

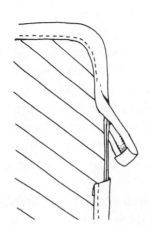

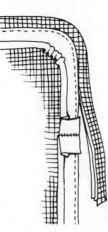

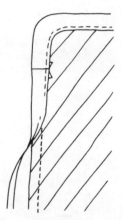

A: Pressing the bias tape in half with 1/16" extra extending on one edge

B: The one-step method

C: Part one of the two-step method

FIGURE 8

D: Part two of the two-step method

folded edges of the tape should be 1/16" longer than the other edge (Figure 8A).

Pin the creased bias tape over the edge of the block, interfacing, and lining. The edge of the tape that is 1/16" longer should be on the *lining* side of the block. Pull the tape slightly as you turn the rounded corners. All the raw edges are encased inside the bias tape. Turn under the ends about ½" where they meet. The ends should butt together. Slipstitch them together. Baste the bias tape in place. Machine stitch from the block side ⅛" from the inner edge (Figure 8B).

The *two-step application* is used for thick or quilted blocks when the edge is more unstable. Working from the lining side, place the crease on one side of the bias tape over the ½" seamline of the block. The right sides are together. Pin around the entire block. Pull the tape slightly around the rounded corners. Turn back ½" where the two ends meet. Slip stitch them together. Machine stitch on the crease of the bias tape around the entire block. Trim the block seam allowance so it is even with the edge of the bias tape (Figure 8C).

Press the bias tape over the raw edges to the right side of the clutch. The bias tape will cover the first stitching done from the lining side. Stitch from the block side ⅛" from the edge of the bias tape (Figure 8D).

FIGURE 9

A: Positioning the tie closure . . .

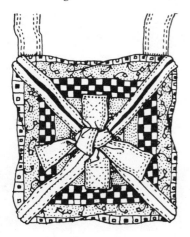

B: and the shoulder strap

The shoulder strap and tie closure:

Cut the ribbon or webbing into two 11" pieces and one 32" piece. You can make your own straps from fabric if you like as shown in Project 3, Figure 15.

Hem one end of each of the 11" tie pieces. Press under ½" on the other ends of the ties and both ends of the shoulder strap. Lay the clutch out flat with the lining side up. Fold the four corners inward so they meet at the center evenly. Press the creases in where they are folded.

Pin and baste the ties in place at the end that is turned under ½", on two opposite sections as shown in Figure 9A. The clutch is closed by tying the two hemmed ends together.

Turn the clutch over. Pin and baste the shoulder strap in position at each folded corner at the top of the clutch below the crease you have pressed (Figure 9B).

Open the clutch out flat. Stitch the ties and shoulder strap in place through the block, interfacing, and lining (Figure 10). Use the box formation of stitching as shown in Project 4, Figure 10. Make sure the shoulder strap is not twisted.

The final stitching:

Working flat with the right side up, fold three corners of the clutch in toward the center. The shoulder straps should be at the top. Stitch the binding together along the edges where the folded sections meet. Use a slipstitch. Your stitches should not go through to the right side of the clutch. Make sure that the bottom of the

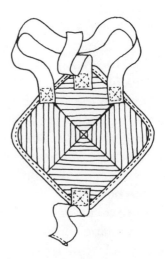

FIGURE 10:
Stitching the tie closure and the shoulder strap to the opened clutch

bag is closed tightly at the corners (Figure 11). Turn the bag right side out and press lightly.

SUGGESTIONS AND SIMPLIFICATIONS

This project has the distinction of being as simple as possible. The lining and/or interfacing could possibly be eliminated; however, this would make the clutch very limp. Omitting these two layers would not really save any time or eliminate any difficult steps, so it's best to make the clutch just as demonstrated.

The shoulder strap could be left off if you prefer carrying an envelope-style purse. This would be especially appropriate for an evening bag.

If you are making the Clever Clutch to go with a specific outfit, use some of the same material in the sample block. I have one clutch made from wool scraps that were left over from all the winter skirts I made last year.

Any of the sample blocks can be used for the Clever Clutch. The life preserver in Block 11 cannot be made with a shoulder strap. Eliminate the cotton cord on the life preserver design. Place the design on the diagonal so it will be right side up on the back of the clutch. The designs in Block 14 must be placed on the sample block diagonally in order to be right side up on the back of the purse.

The Clever Clutch makes a good traveling bag for stockings or small items. Make it on a smaller scale, eliminate the final stitching and use it as a perfect needle case. Sew snaps inside on each corner to hold the needle case closed.

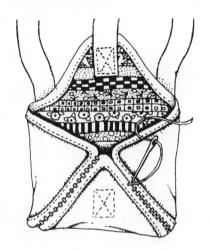

FIGURE 11:
Slipstitching the edges of the clutch together from the inside

CHAPTER EIGHT

Block 8

Translucent Appliqué

This appliqué technique is done in the same way as simple appliqué. The only difference is that you use sheer fabrics such as organdy. Different colors of organdy are placed on top of each other so that areas of the design overlap. This overlapping creates a delicate, transparent moiré pattern. This is a decorative, irregular, wave-like design that resembles a wood grain. Test this by holding two pieces of white organdy together near a light.

The layering of the different colors of organdy also produces a change in color. For example: yellow placed over red makes light orange. In reverse, red placed over yellow makes dark orange. This is a beautiful, subtle technique that is enhanced by lighting. The moiré patterns move, and the colors change with the light.

For this block, the appliquéd pieces are fused to a large square of organdy with a fabric fuser.

No raw edges are turned under. This process allows you to cut out easily tricky, intricate shaped pieces that you could not use if you had to turn under the raw edges. The fabric fuser seals the raw edges and prevents them from fraying.

Hand or machine stitching is added to each shape. This outlines and accentuates each color in the design like leading in a stained-glass window.

Examine different colors and fabrics carefully before using them. Organdy that is 100 percent cotton is best. It is stiff and firmly woven so it can be cut and handled easily. If you don't find the colors you want, don't worry; organdy dyes easily and quickly. Get a yard or so extra of white organdy. Cut it into several pieces. Dye them whatever colors you like. Rinse them well after dying, and iron each piece dry on an *old* towel to remove any excess color. Avoid slippery, loosely woven fabrics. Some sheer synthetics unravel instantly after they're cut.

SUPPLIES *(enough for one sample block)*

¼ yard each of four different colors of organdy

> If you cannot find organdy in the colors you would like, buy 1 yard of white organdy and dye it yourself.

½ yard white organdy

> This is for the background square. It could also be a pale pastel color.

½ yard fabric fuser

Embroidery floss

> This is for hand embroidering the edge of the leaves. Brown is a likely color. If you plan to embroider by machine, get regular thread in a good color.

Thread to match the organdy background

Plain paper

> You need two 15″ squares.

DIRECTIONS

Dying your own organdy:

It is sometimes very difficult to find organdy in nice colors. Don't be afraid to dye your own. It's quite simple. Skip this section if you were able to find four colors or organdy.

Buy 1 yard of white organdy. Pick out four colors of fabric dye. My sample was done with yellow, orange, red, and brown.

Cut the organdy into four 18″ squares. Whey dying fabrics, begin with the lightest color. This prevents acci-

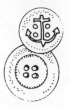

dental miscoloring when a dark color dye was used in the dye pot first. It only takes a few drops of a dark color to make light colors look dirty.

Cut about eight test strips from the leftover organdy. They should each be about ½" x 2". Always test the color of the dye bath before submerging your fabric.

Make a weak solution of the yellow dye and water in an *old* pot that you no longer use for cooking. Enamel pans from the dime store are perfect and are not badly stained by the dye. The larger the amount of fabric you are dying, the larger the dye pot should be. Check the package for specifics.

Heat and stir the mixture. You only need about two cups of dye solution. You can add the dye a few grains at a time until you have the color intensity you want. It's much easier to store leftover dye when it's left in the package. Don't overdo the amount. Test the color with a test strip. Dry the test strip with your iron. Colors will dry lighter. Add more dye if you want a darker color.

Boil the dye bath. In plain water, wet one of the organdy squares completely. Thoroughly wet fabric assures even dying. Squeeze out excess water. Drop the square into the dye. It should be in a loosely crushed ball. Stir the dye continuously. Air bubbles trapped in the fabric cause white spots. Pockets of concentrated dye cause dark spots.

When the color is slightly stronger than desired, plunge the fabric into a sink full of cold water. Rinsing removes some of the dye, and the fabric will be lighter when it is dry. Rinse the fabric until the water runs clear. Squeeze the excess water out.

Place several layers of newspaper and then an *old* towel over your ironing board. Open the dyed square on the towel. Cover it with heavy brown paper or another towel. Use the "cotton" heat setting on your iron. Iron the organdy dry. The towels and paper will collect any water or excess dye. Be careful when ironing paper; don't allow the iron to scorch it. If the color is not strong enough, you can repeat the dying process. Iron the towels completely dry or use fresh paper to prevent staining on the next color. Also remove any dye from the surface of the iron before tackling the next color.

Dye the three remaining squares in the same way. Work from the lightest color to the darkest. For example: yellow, orange, red, and then brown.

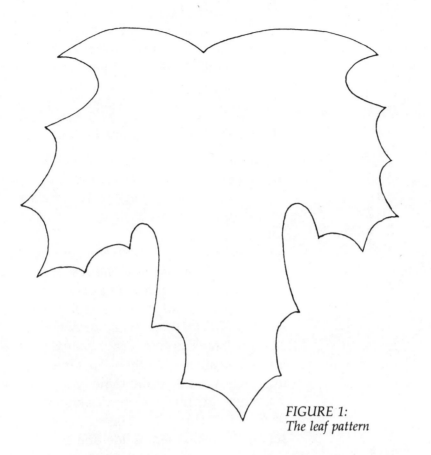

FIGURE 1:
The leaf pattern

Cutting:

Trace the leaf pattern in Figure 1 onto a piece of plain paper. Working flat, pin one of the pieces of colored organdy over the leaf pattern. Trace the leaf directly onto the organdy using a pencil (Figure 2). Move the pattern and trace the second leaf close to the first in the same way. Draw the leaves accurately so that they all look the same. You will need two leaves from each of the four colors. These eight leaves will complete one sample block. Trace all the leaves you need from each color at one time.

Cut one square of organdy around the leaves you have traced. Pin this square to a square of the fabric fuser that is about the same size. Pin the two pieces together along the outside edge.

Make long basting stitches around the inside of each leaf. This will hold the fuser to the leaves after they have been cut out. Cut the leaves out on the lines with very sharp scissors. You will be cutting the two layers

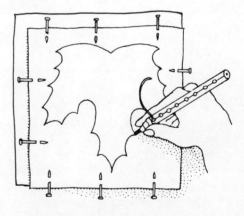

FIGURE 2:
Drawing a leaf on an organdy square. The paper pattern is underneath

out at the same time so they will be identical (Figure 3). Handle them carefully. Try not to rough up the raw edges after they have been cut. Store them like tortillas—with a piece of paper between each leaf.

Cut a 15″ square from the white organdy. This is the background for the leaf design.

Making the wreath layout:

Cut out a 15″ square from plain paper. Fold it in half, then quarters, then eighths. Open it up and draw pencil lines on the foldlines. They will all intersect at the center of the square. Draw a 4″ circle in the center of the square.

Cut out the leaf pattern. Using the circle and the lines as guides, position eight leaves in a wreath layout. *Lightly* draw around the outside of the pattern. Move the pattern around to the next line and draw another leaf. Complete the wreath drawing, and make any changes if the placement isn't quite right. The tips of the leaves will all point in the same direction. The lines will intersect each leaf at the same location (Figure 4).

Go over the final wreath design with a felt tip pen or dark pencil. This doesn't need to be beautiful because it serves as a placement guide only.

Working on an ironing board, pin the organdy square on top of the placement guide. Match and pin the edges together.

Beginning with the lightest color leaves, place them in position exactly on top of the wreath design that you drew (Figure 5).

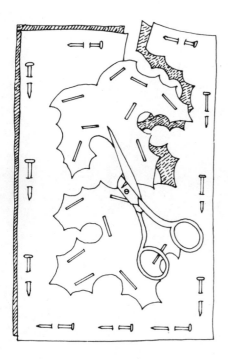

FIGURE 3:
Cutting out the leaves from the organdy basted to the fabric fuser

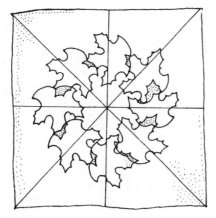

FIGURE 4:
Drawing the leaves in a wreath design on paper

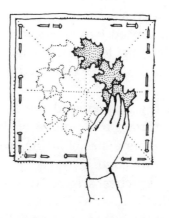

FIGURE 5:
Positioning the organdy leaves on the background square that is pinned over the paper layout

Experiment with overlapping the different colored leaves in different ways. The same color organdy will look different depending on whether it is on top or underneath another color. When you have made the color layout that you like best, pin all the leaves in position. Carefully remove the basting so it doesn't get fused in permanently. Fuse each leaf in place with your iron. Cover the wreath with paper or muslin to prevent the fuser from gumming up your iron (Figure 6).

The raw edges of each leaf are now outlined with stitching. This makes the edges more decorative and less fragile.

Using embroidery floss, do the blanket stitch if you are working by hand. If you have a zigzag stitch on your machine, adjust it so that the stitches are very close together. Work the machine satin stitch or the blanket stitch by hand around each leaf (Figure 7). Put the finished embroidery face down on a terry cloth towel, and iron from the wrong side. This protects the embroidery from being smashed by the iron.

This block is ready to use for the Creative Café Curtains in the next part of the chapter. Each block will be 14" wide when it is finished. Measure your window and make as many blocks as needed to cross the window. One is probably perfect for the bathroom. The kitchen window might need three or four blocks.

This block is translucent. If you want to use is for any project other than the curtains, it must be backed with a 15" square of plain fabric. Try several colors and white to see what looks best. The block can be quilted after it is backed. Make the outline stitch around the outside and inside of the wreath. You don't need to quilt each leaf separately unless you want to.

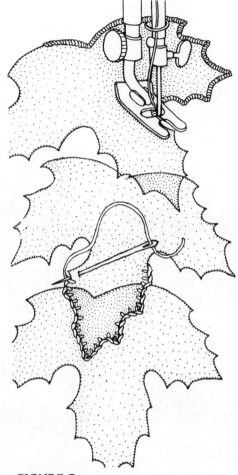

FIGURE 7:
Covering the raw edges of each leaf with either machine or hand embroidery

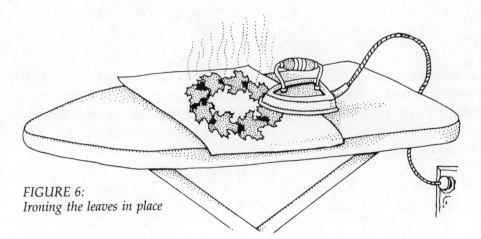

FIGURE 6:
Ironing the leaves in place

Project 8

Creative Café Curtains

This project uses *four* blocks or as many as are needed to fit across your window. They should *not* be quilted. These curtains were inspired by a special type of Japanese shop curtains called *noren*. These are horizontally-hung banners placed outside a store to indicate what is sold inside. Restaurants use them to advertise what style of food/cooking is used. Each block is made into a separate banner by adding a lining and three loops. The blocks are then hung side by side on a rod or wooden dowel.

   The same banner could also be used as a wall hanging, room divider, or valence. Use one block to hang in the bathroom window or a dozen blocks for a contemporary canopy hung like ship's flags over your bed.

SUPPLIES *(enough for one sample block)*

One unquilted sample block for each curtain

> You need one curtain for every 14 inches of window you wish to cross.

½ yard backing fabric

> This should be the same type of fabric as the sample block. It does not need to be the same color.

Thread

> It should match the backing fabric.

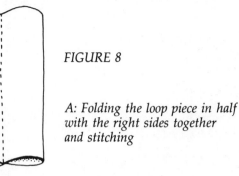

FIGURE 8

A: Folding the loop piece in half with the right sides together and stitching

DIRECTIONS

Cutting:

Cut a 15″ square from the backing fabric. The loop pieces measure 4½″ x 7″. Cut three loops for each block that you are using.

Making the loops:

Fold the loop pieces in half lengthwise with the right sides together. Pin and sew a seam ½″ from the matched raw edges (Figure 8A).

Trim the seam to ¼″, and turn the piece right side out. Press the loop flat so that the seam is on one side of the piece (Figure 8B). Fold the loop crosswise, bringing the raw edges together. Pin the ends together evenly (Figure 8C). Make all the loops at one time.

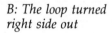

B: The loop turned right side out

C: Folding the loop in half crosswise

Attaching the loops to the block:

Place three loops at the top edge of the right side of the block matching the raw edges. Two of the loops should be ¾″ from the sides of the block. The third loop is in the middle of the first two (Figure 9).

Baste the loops in place ½″ from the raw edges. Make sure the loops are straight and even. The seam allowance in each loop should go in the same direction if you are using translucent fabric.

FIGURE 9:
Positioning the three loops on the sample block along the top edge

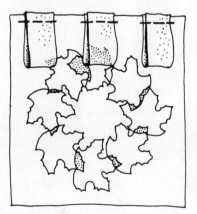

The backing square:

Put the backing square on top of the block. The right sides will be together, and the loops are between the block and the backing. Pin block and backing together ½″ from the edges on all the sides. Leave a 6″ opening on

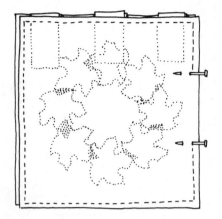

FIGURE 10:
Putting the backing square on top
of the sample block with the
loops inside, and leaving an opening
for turning

one side, not the bottom. Do not catch the *sides* of the loops in the seams (Figure 10).

Trim the seams to ¼". Trim the corners as shown in Project 1, Figure 5. Turn the curtain right side out through the opening. Flatten the seam edges on all four sides of the block by rolling them between your fingers and pressing.

Turn in the seam allowances at the 6" opening. Close the opening invisibly with the slipstich. Press the entire curtain flat except don't crease the loops. Leave them rounded at the top so they will hang nicely over the curtain rod.

SUGGESTIONS

This project makes a good banner or wall hanging as well as curtains. Sew fringe to the bottom edge. Attach several different blocks together vertically to make a long, totem-pole-style room divider.

These curtains can become pillows also. Make four curtains and stuff them before you close the side opening. Use a wooden dowel to hang them on the wall behind your studio couch or day bed. When placed at the right height, they make perfect backrests.

No matter how you use them, each individual curtain unit can be different. Tell a story with picture appliqué, or write a name putting one giant letter on each banner.

SIMPLIFICATION

Loops: Instead of making your own loops from fabric, cut 7" lengths of 1½" or 2" wide ribbon. Baste the ends of the three loops together. Position them at the top of each block in the same manner as with the fabric loops.

CHAPTER NINE

Block 9 # Cut-away Appliqué

This technique is often called reverse appliqué. Whatever you call it, it is made exactly as its name implies—by subtracting layers of fabric. You begin with as many as twelve different colors of broadcloth. These pieces are all the same size and layered evenly.

Geometric and linear design are drawn on the top layer. A tiny seam allowance is marked. You then cut away the indicated portions of the design revealing the second color beneath.

As each layer is cut away, seam allowances are turned under, and the edges are stitched down by hand using the overhand stitch. In this way, you "carve" through the layers one at a time, revealing a multicolored design. It has a thick, somewhat stiff, *hand-finished* (as opposed to "homemade") look.

Depending on the number of layers and the complexity of the design, this technique requires a concentration of detailed work in a relatively small area. The result is row after row of colored halos that radiate from a dark center.

For this block select three bright colors. For the bottom layer choose a dark color like black, navy, or dark brown.

SUPPLIES *(enough for one sample block)*

½ yard each of four different colors of broadcloth

Get three bright colors that look good together. The fourth color should be a dark accent color.

Thread

Get thread to match the three bright colors of broadcloth.

Cardboard 8″ x 8″

You need about an 8″ square for making templates.

DIRECTIONS

Cutting:

Cut a 15″ square from each of the four colors of broadcloth.

Making the templates:

Transfer the templates from Figure 1 to the cardboard square. Cut out both pieces.

Transferring the design to the fabric:

Layer the four colors of fabric in the order that looks best. You may want to cut small pieces from the leftover fabric to experiment. Try putting the colors next to each other in different orders. The darkest color should always be on the bottom. This is because it may show through or "dirty" one of the light-colored layers. Traditionally it was used on the bottom to give the illusion of depth.

FIGURE 1:
The templates

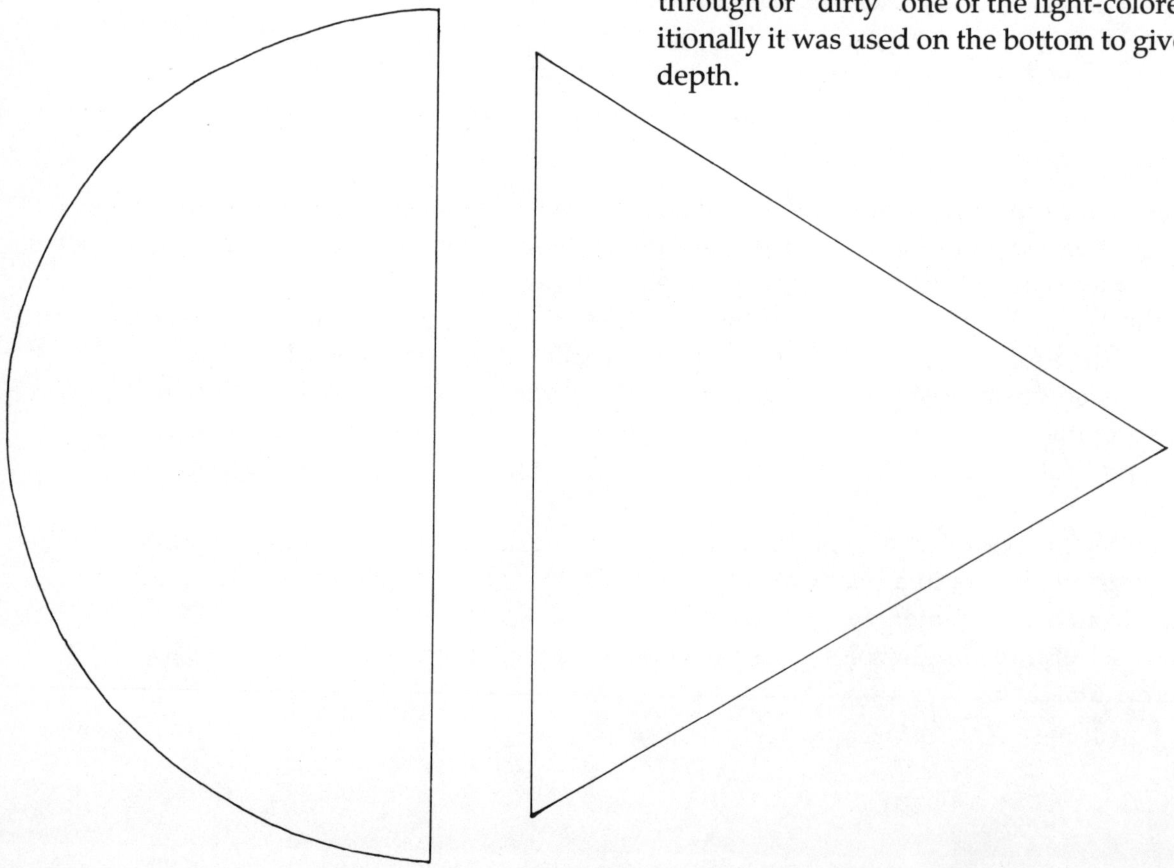

Layer the four squares in the order that you have selected. Match the raw edges and baste them together along the outer edges (Figure 2). Make sure that all the layers are smooth and flat.

Locate the exact center of the squares, and mark it on the top piece of fabric with a chalk dot. Measure down 7½" on two opposite sides of the squares. Put a mark at this point on both sides. Draw a chalk line across the square that goes through the center dot and connects the two marks, dividing the block in half.

Baste across the square on this line through all four thicknesses of fabric. Position the triangular template on the fabric so that the point is ½" away from the center dot. One side of the triangle is ¼" away from and parallel to the basting line. Draw around the template with chalk or pencil. Repeat this on the other side of the basting line. The two triangles should be spaced ½" apart and ½" from the center dot.

Draw two more triangles in the same way on the opposite side of the center dot. Fill in the spaces between the two pairs of triangles with a single triangle. All six triangles are ½" from the center dot and ½" apart from one another.

Center the half-circle template on the outside of each triangle. It should be ½" away from the triangle. The flat side of the template is longer than the outer side of the triangle. Center the half circle so approximately ¼" extends on both sides beyond the corners of the triangle. Draw the half circles around the six triangles in this manner (Figure 3).

Baste ¼" away from all the chalk lines you have drawn. The chalk lines are represented by a solid line on the illustration (Figure 4). This secures all the fabrics together so that you can cut through the layers without any danger of shifting or slipping.

Cutting through the first layer:

The templates are used over and over to draw each layer as you cut through the different colors. They are trimmed smaller each time to make a series of concentric shapes.

Draw a line ¼" inside the cut edges of *both* the triangle and the half circle templates. Be accurate; a ⅛" error will make a difference! Trim both templates down on this line. This makes them ¼" smaller on all sides.

Center the new, smaller, templates inside the original lines that you drew. Draw around each template. This

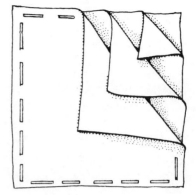

FIGURE 2:
Layering the four colors of fabric

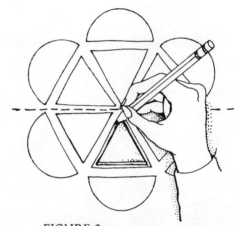

FIGURE 3:
*Laying out the design
using the templates*

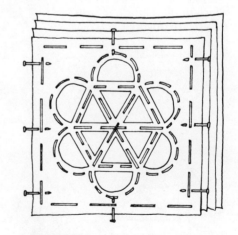

FIGURE 4:
*Basting the layers of fabric together
around the design*

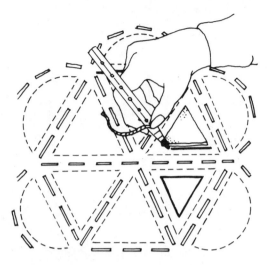

FIGURE 5:
*Drawing the cutting line
with a trimmed template*

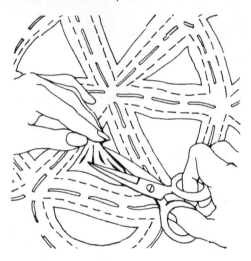

FIGURE 6:
*Pinching the fabric and cutting
into the first layer*

second line made from the new size template should be ¼″ away from the first line on all sides. The folding line is shown as a dotted line in the illustrations. The solid line is the cutting line (Figure 5).

Pinch the top layer of fabric in the middle of the second triangle. Make sure that you have only one layer by rolling the fabric between your fingers (Figure 6).

Use sharp, pointed embroidery scissors to snip a small slash inside the second triangle. Be very careful not to cut into the next color fabric.

Cut the second triangle out on the cutting line that you drew with the trimmed template (Figure 7). This now exposes the next color. Repeat this on all the triangles. Cut the inner half-circles out in the same way that you did the triangles.

Carefully clip the corners of the triangle outward to 1/16″ from the first line. Do not go past the foldline! Clip the two corners and the curve of the half circle in the same way (Figure 8). The curve of the half circle will need to be clipped at ½″ intervals.

Thread a needle in the color that matches the top layer. Use the point of the needle to tuck under the cut edges of the first layer. Use your thumbnail to hold the edges tightly while sewing. Begin in one corner, and fold under ¼″ of fabric up to the foldline. Pin it in place (Figure 8). Continue tucking the edge under around the entire shape. Use as few pins as necessary. Handle the cut edges as little as possible.

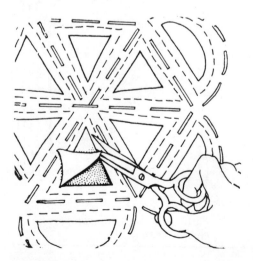

FIGURE 7:
*Exposing the second color
by cutting on the line*

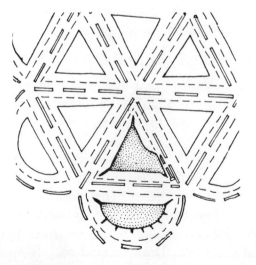

FIGURE 8:
*Clipping the corners and curves.
Turning the edges back
to the foldline*

After all the edges are tucked inside, use over-hand stitches spaced ⅛" to ¼" apart to sew the folded edge down. Make your stitches very close together. The corners need to be secured very well. Make three or four stitches that radiate out from each corner (Figure 9). Use your needle to pull back the corners and make them sharp and pointed.

Repeat this process in each triangle and half circle. The first layer should be completely done before you cut into the second layer because the size of the template will be trimmed down to do the second layer. Press the block flat.

Cutting through the second layer:

Use the templates as they are. Center them on the second color. Draw a line around them inside each triangle and half circle. This is the foldline. It is ¼" away from the stitching of the first layer.

Draw a line on the templates ¼" away from the outer edge as you did before. Trim ¼" off of both templates for the second time. Center them inside the foldlines you have just drawn, and draw around them. This is the cutting line. It should be ¼" from the foldline.

Pinch the center of the shape and cut on the cutting line, revealing the third color layer (Figure 10).

Tuck the second layer under on the foldlines with your needle as you did on the first layer. Stitch the folded edges of the second layer in place and secure the corners with matching thread (Figure 11). Repeat this on all the other triangles and half circles. Press the block flat.

Cutting through the third layer:

Use the templates just as they are. Center them on the third color layer inside each shape and draw a line around them. This is the foldline. It should be ¼" away from the stitching of the second layer.

Trim the template, once again, to ¼" inside the outer edges. Center this smaller template inside the foldlines and draw around it. This is the last cutting line. Cut out along the cutting line by pinching and separating the layers as you did before. This reveals the fourth color layer.

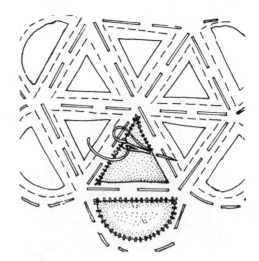

FIGURE 9:
Stitching the first layer down with the overhand stitch

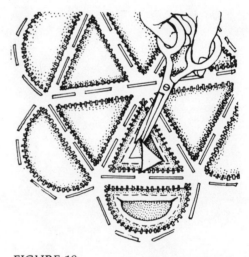

FIGURE 10:
Cutting into the second layer on the cutting line

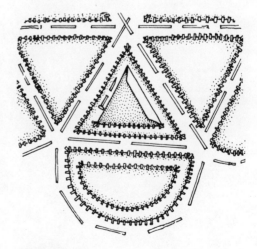

FIGURE 11:
Turning under the second layer on the foldline

FIGURE 12:
*The completed sample block
with all four layers exposed*

Clip the corners, and tuck under the raw edges up to foldlines. Stitch and secure the corners as before in matching thread (Figure 12). Repeat this process in all the other triangles and half circles. Press the block flat.

The block is now ready to use for the Super Sewing Box in the second part of this chapter.

This block is very thick so it doesn't need to be quilted. It can be used just as it is for a project that calls for a quilted block.

This technique lends itself best to geometric designs. Sharply curved and tiny-angled shapes are more difficult to do well. Try layering more than four colors. It is possible to cut through two colors at a time. This changes the sequence of the colors by skipping over one color.

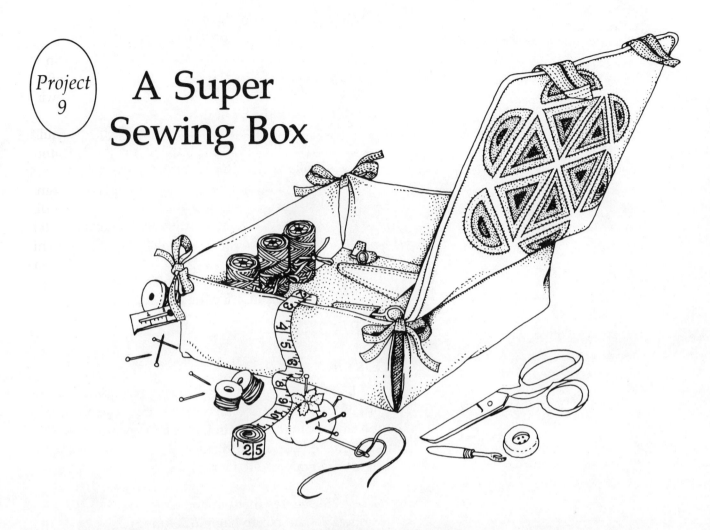

Project 9

A Super Sewing Box

This project uses *one* block. It should be quilted or thick such as the Cut-away Appliqué block. This block forms the lid of a collapsible cloth sewing organizer. There are individual pockets for all your supplies. It hangs up with everything in view while you are working. When you're finished, it packs up neatly, hiding unfinished projects and clutter without a clue to the contents!

SUPPLIES

One sample block
> Use a block that is made of many layers such as the Cut-away Appliqué, or quilt any other sample block. It should be thicker and sturdier than a plain piece of fabric.

2½ yards of broadcloth or medium weight fabric
> This is for the construction of the box and pockets. Get something that goes well with the sample block.

3 yards of ½" wide bias tape
> Make ties inside the box for spools of thread from this. Get a matching or accent color.

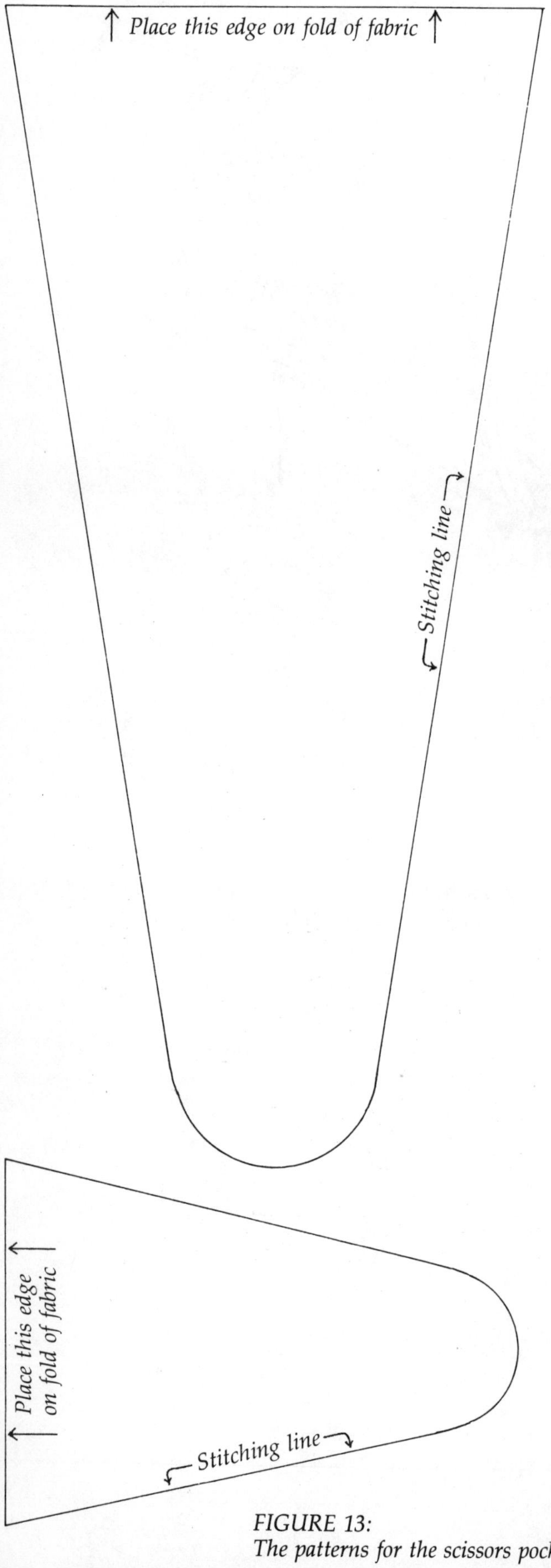

↑ *Place this edge on fold of fabric* ↑

← *Stitching line* →

← *Place this edge on fold of fabric* ←

← *Stitching line* →

FIGURE 13:
The patterns for the scissors pockets

2½ yards of 1″ wide bias tape

Make the ties on the corners of the box from this width. Get the same color as the ½″ bias tape.

½ yard of ¼″ elastic

1½ yards of ¼″ piping

This is sewn around the sample block. Match either the bias tape or the fabric. If you want to make your own matching piping, get one extra yard of fabric and 1½ yards of cotton cording.

Thread

Get two colors. One should match the bias tape, and one should match the fabric.

Heavy cardboard

Get a piece that is about 30″ square. You'll cut pieces from it for the box supports.

DIRECTIONS

Cutting:

All of the pieces for the box are cut from the 2½ yards of fabric. Measure the pieces and draw them right on the fabric. Cut them out in the order they are given. The straight edges should follow the lengthwise or crosswise grain of the fabric.

two 25″ squares (bottom and side)
one 15″ x 20″ (scrap bag/block lining)
one 6″ x 12″ (facing for scrap bag)
one 5″ x 25″ (notions pocket)

two scissors pockets (Figure 13 contains patterns in two sizes). The patterns do not contain seam allowances. Add a ½″ seam allowance to the sides and curved bottom of both pocket patterns before cutting.

Making the box lid:

Decide which side of the sample block should be the top, and mark it along the raw edge. Baste all the raw edges of the block together.

Apply piping to the two sides and bottom edges on the right side of the block. Project 2, Figure 7, gives instructions for applying piping to raw edges and around corners (Figure 14).

Cut two 8″ lengths of 1″ wide bias tape for the tabs. Press the creased edges together lengthwise. Edgestitch the two creases together. Edgestitch the folded edge. Make a second row of stitching ⅛″ away from each row of edgestitching. Fold each strip as shown in Figure 15A.

Sew the folded strips together by hand, using an invisible slipstitch. This is the right side of the tabs. Secure the stitching 2″ from the matched raw edges. Press the tab flat. Hand or machine stitch across the base of the triangle that is formed. This forms a 1¼″ opening for the button (Figure 15B).

Position the two tabs on top of the piping 3″ from the sides of the sample block. Match the raw edges and baste them in place. Make sure that the right sides of the tabs are against the right sides of the block (Figure 14).

Hem the 6″ x 12″ scrap bag facing on the two long sides and one short side. Fold the scrap bag facing in half lengthwise. Crease this halfway line with your iron. Make a mark on the crease that is 9″ from one raw edge. Draw a parallel line on both sides of the crease that is ½″ away from the crease. These two lines should extend 8″ from the unhemmed side of the facing. Connect these two lines with a round end so that it is a test tube shape. Use a compass or draw around a spool of thread to make the half-circle bottom.

Crease the 15″ x 20″ scrap bag piece in half vertically. With right sides together, place the facing on top of the scrap bag piece. Match the raw edges and the center creaselines. Pin and stitch the two layers together on the test-tube-shaped line you drew. Trim the fabric away inside the test tube slot opening so that it is ¼″ away from the stitching (Figure 16A).

Turn the facing through the slot opening so that the wrong sides are together. Press the facing flat. Make two rows of top stitching around the slot opening.

Measure 2″ in toward the slot opening on both ends of the top edge of the scrap bag piece. Make marks. Draw a line from each lower corner of the piece to these marks. Cut on these lines (Figure 16B). Gather the lower, longer edge of this trapezoid shape to 15″.

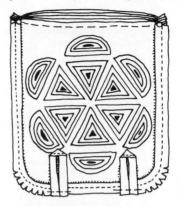

FIGURE 14:
*Applying the piping
to the sample block,
and placing the button loops*

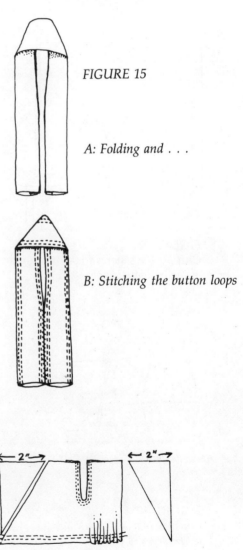

FIGURE 15

A: Folding and . . .

B: Stitching the button loops

FIGURE 16

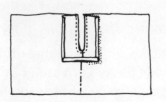

*A: Stitching the facing
to the scrap bag piece*

*B: Turning the facing and topstitching,
cutting both sides of the rectangle
to form a trapezoid,
and gathering the bottom edge*

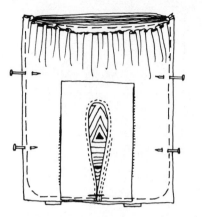

FIGURE 17:
Joining the scrap bag and the sample block

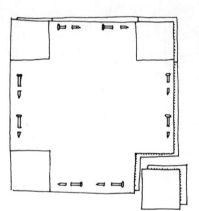

FIGURE 18:
Cutting the squares from each corner of the bottom/side piece

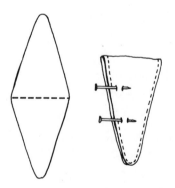

FIGURE 19:
Construction of the scissors pockets

Place the scrap bag over the sample block with right sides together. Match all the raw edges. Bring the two edges of the slot opening together at the center of the block. Pin and baste the scrap bag to the sample block on the sides and bottom. The top remains open. Stitch the three sides close to the piping with a zipper foot. The scrap bag facing and the tabs will be attached at the same time. Leave the top gathered end unstitched (Figure 17).

The box bottom and sides:

Working flat, pin the two 25" squares together evenly. Draw a perfect 4½" square in each corner on the top piece. Cut the squares out of each corner. Make sure the pieces are identical (Figure 18).

The scissors pockets:

There are two patterns in Figure 13 for the scissors pockets. The large one is for cutting shears. The smaller one is for embroidery scissors. They are assembled and attached in the same way. You may want to make an additional pocket for pinking shears or any other scissors you have. Save the large pattern after you have used it to make a button later.

Fold each pocket in half along the foldline. The right sides must be together. Match the edges as shown in Figure 19, leaving a 3" opening along one side. Stitch ½" from the raw edges. Trim and turn each pocket right side out and press it flat.

Indicate the top edge of *one* of the bottom/side pieces. Measure 8" up from the lowest edge of the piece and 8" in from the left side. Mark these spots with pins. Position the large scissor pocket so that the pointed bottom is at this spot. Pin, baste, and stitch the pocket in place, making sure it is vertical. Make two rows of stitching close to the edge. Repeat this with the smaller scissor pocket. The smaller one is about 2" to the right of the larger one.

Making the notions pocket:

Make a casing in one of the 25" edges of the notions pocket piece. Turn under ¼" on the raw edge. Turn this edge down ½". Stitch the hem by machine and edge-stitch the fold. Cut a 13" piece from the ¼" elastic. Insert it into the casing using a safety pin. Stitch across the elastic at both ends of the casing (Figure 20).

Press under ½" on the two 5" ends of the notions pocket. Gather the lower raw edge to 12".

Draw a chalk line connecting the inner corners of the two cut-out 4½" squares at the top of the bottom/side piece (Figure 21A).

With the wrong side of the notions pocket up, place the gathered edge along this line on the bottom/side piece. The seamline of the pocket should be ½" below the chalk line. The gathered raw edge will be even with the chalk line. Center the pocket so that it is 1½" from the beginning of the chalk line on both sides. Pin, baste, and stitch the pocket along this line (Figure 21B).

Press the notions pocket up toward the top of the bottom/side piece. Pin the folded side edges so they are vertical. They will be 1½" in from the side edges. Stitch the side edges with two rows of machine stitching squared off at both ends (Figure 21C).

The thread ties:

Press a 3 yard piece of ½" wide bias tape in half lengthwise. Match the long folded edges and make one row of machine stitching down the middle. The stitched piece will be ¼" wide. Cut this into six 18" pieces. Make a knot close to each cut end so that the ends don't get ragged looking. Find the center of each piece and mark it with a pin.

Position three ties on the right and the lower sections of the bottom/side piece as shown in Figure 22. The center of each piece is stitched down with a narrow rectangle of stitching. The ties are all 2½" from and parallel to the outer edges of the bottom/side piece. Space them apart equally. Tie them all in bows so they don't flop around.

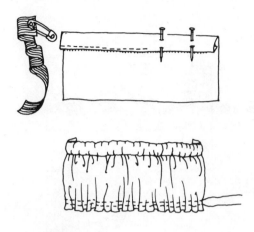

FIGURE 20:
Construction of the notions pocket

FIGURE 21

A: Drawing a line on the bottom side piece

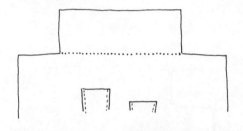

B: Positioning the notions pocket

C: Flipping the notions pocket up into place and stitching the sides

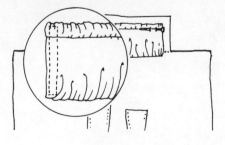

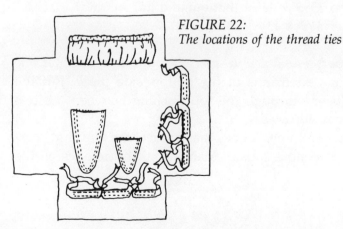

FIGURE 22:
The locations of the thread ties

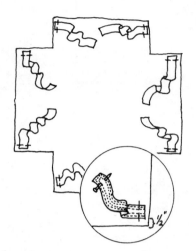

FIGURE 23:
The locations of the corner ties

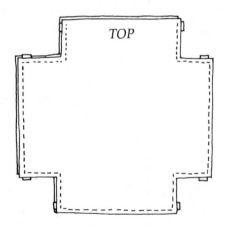

FIGURE 24:
Joining the two bottom/side pieces

The corner ties:

The box is made collapsible by ties that are attached to each corner. Cut eight 9″ pieces of 1″ wide bias tape. Hem one end, and press the tape in half as shown in Project 7, Figure 8A. Top stitch each tie with two or four rows of top stitching.

Place one tie at each corner of the bottom/side piece as shown in Figure 23. Match the raw end of each tie with the raw edge where the 4½″ squares were cut out. Each tie should be ½″ away from the outermost sides of the bottom/side piece. Baste the ties in place. Pin each tie in toward the center so the ends will not flop around.

Assembling the bottom/side pieces:

Put the plain bottom/side on top of the one with the pockets and ties. Match all the outer raw edges. Pin and baste them together using a ½″ seam allowance. Do not baste the *top* edge closed.

The corner ties will be secured in this seam. Make sure that *only* the *raw ends* of the corner ties are caught in the seam. Do not catch the sides or hemmed ends of the ties in this seam. Watch out for stray ties sticking out between the two large pieces. Pin and keep all the tie ends inside the two pieces. Machine stitch on top of the basting. Be certain not to close the top edge (Figure 24).

Trim the edges and corners of the two bottom/side pieces to ¼″. Clip the inward corners to ⅛″ from the stitching. Turn the two pieces right side out through the top opening. Carefully pull out each corner by pulling the corner ties. Flatten the seamed edges and press the entire bottom/side piece. Edgestitch around the entire piece stopping 2″ from the top opening. Your stitches should be as close to the edge as possible.

Inserting the cardboard supports:

Cut your cardboard into the following shapes:

two 13½″ x 13½″ (bottom and lid)
four 4½″ x 13½″ (four sides)

Insert a 4½″ x 13½″ piece into the two side and one bottom extensions of the bottom/side piece. Put the cardboard through the top opening between the two bottom/side pieces.

Draw four chalk lines that connect the four inner corners making a square. Machine stitch the lines on the side and bottom extensions after you have inserted each piece of cardboard. Use a zipper foot to stitch close to the cardboard rectangles.

After the sides and lower extensions have the cardboard stitched in, insert a 13½" x 13½" into the center. Stitch it in place with a zipper foot just beneath the gathers of the notions pocket. Fill the top extension with the last 4½" x 13½" piece. Baste the top opening closed, close to the cardboard (Figure 25).

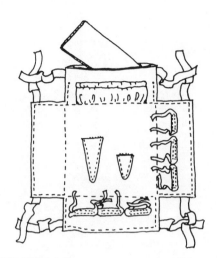

FIGURE 25:
Inserting the last cardboard support

Attaching the lid to the box:

Match the top raw edges of the bottom/side piece to the raw edges of the sample block. Pin and baste these two edges together. Do not baste the gathered scrap bag into this stitching. The piping will extend beyond the matched edges. Stitch through all of these thicknesses by machine. Secure the ends well (Figure 26). Trim the seam evenly to ¼". Insert the last 13½" x 13½" square into the lid.

Tuck under ½" along the gathered edge of the scrap bag. Press the raw edges of the bottom/side piece up toward the lid. Cover the raw edges with the gathered edge. Use the slipstitch to sew the gathered edge to the stitching line. Distribute the gathers evenly and stitch them in place securely (Figure 27).

FIGURE 26:
Stitching the lid to the bottom/side piece

Toggle button closures:

Use the pattern for the large scissor pocket to make the toggle buttons. Trim off ½" on the outer edges of the

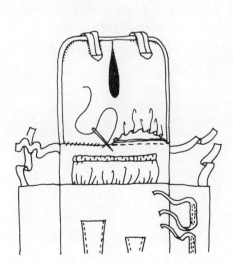

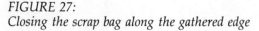

FIGURE 27:
Closing the scrap bag along the gathered edge

FIGURE 28

A: *Constructing the button piece*

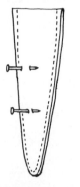

B: *Rolling the button piece into a toggle button*

pattern. Cut two pieces from the fabric. Fold them, stitch and turn them just as you did the scissor pocket. Press each completed piece flat (Figure 28A).

Beginning at the straight edge, roll the fabric triangle. Roll slowly, centering each revolution of fabric. The point of the triangle is the center of the button. Slipstitch it in place (Figure 28B).

Close the box by tying all the corner ties. Put the lid down. Mark the positions for the buttons on the outside of the box. Sew them in place by hand.

SUGGESTIONS AND SIMPLIFICATIONS

The Super Sewing Box can't be simplified without changing the way it functions. I don't recommend that you eliminate any of the parts if you plan to use it as a sewing box. You will need all the pockets for your scissors and notions.

The same design could be made on a smaller scale as an organizer for cosmetics or any other small objects that end up scattered all over your home. Eliminate the thread ties and sew elasticized notions pockets on all four sides of the box. It would be perfect for barrettes, hair ribbons, scarves, etcetera.

The block that you use for the lid of the box is very important. Decide where you want to keep the box. Make a block for the lid using a technique and colors that will make it a real eye-catcher. Match or accent the decor of the room it will be placed in.

The box could be made with a printed fabric or a different color of lining if you like. Cut one of the 25" squares from another fabric. Don't forget to put two hooks on the wall near your sewing area. They should be the same distance apart as the button loops on the lid of the box. Hang your sewing box up on the wall while you're working. Leave the lowest side section tied at the corners to form a small shelf for your thimble and pin cushion.

CHAPTER TEN

$\left(\begin{array}{c} Block \\ 10 \end{array}\right)$ Lacy Appliqué

This form of appliqué, like all the other types, uses the principle of applying a cut-out shape to a piece of background fabric. This technique originates in Hawaii, and when quilted, it is sometimes called Hawaiian quilting.

A snowflake-like shape is cut from a color that contrasts vividly with the background color. The appliquéd piece is almost as large as the background piece so that almost an equal amount of each color is visible.

The appliquéd shape is basted into position on the background. It can be secured in place by hand or with a machine satin stitch.

For this block select tightly woven fabrics that won't fray easily. Choose two solid colors that you like together. You can use matching thread or an accent color. If you are handstitching the edges, a matching color will look best. After the design is appliquéd, the motif and background are then quilted by hand or machine using the echo quilting method.

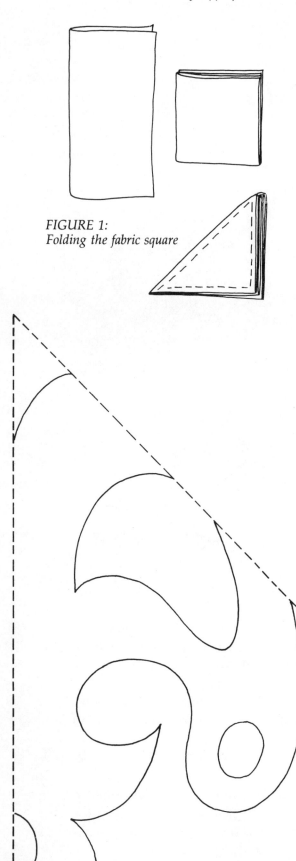

FIGURE 1:
Folding the fabric square

SUPPLIES (*enough for one sample block*)

½ yard each of broadcloth in two solid colors

Pick out two contrasting colors that look good together. If you plan to use a light color on top of a dark color, check to make sure that the light color is opaque enough.

½ yard of thin quilt batting or fleece

½ yard of muslin

Thread

Get a spool to match each color of broadcloth. It will be used for quilting and appliqué.

DIRECTIONS

Cutting:

Cut a 15″ square from each color of broadcloth, from the muslin, and from the batting.

Preparing the appliqué:

Decide which color of broadcloth is to be appliquéd on top of the other. Fold the appliqué piece in half. Crease with the iron. Fold it into quarters and then eighths, pressing each crease. Baste all of the edges together. Make sure the piece is folded and creased accurately (Figure 1).

Transfer the pattern in Figure 2 to a piece of cardboard. Cut it out carefully. The dotted lines on the pattern show you how to position the pattern on the folded fabric.

FIGURE 2:
The pattern

Hold the pattern in place on the folded fabric. Carefully draw around each part of the pattern. Don't move it until you have completely finished drawing (Figure 3).

Make some additional basting lines through all thicknesses of the fabric. They should be just inside the design lines that you drew. This holds the fabric layers together while you are cutting.

Cut the design out on the lines that you have drawn. Cut evenly through all the thicknesses of fabric. Carefully remove the basting stitches. Separate the layers cautiously. Try not to handle the raw edges roughly.

Fold the other broadcloth square into fourths. Press the creases in, and then open it. Center the appliqué cut-out on top of the plain square. Match the creases to make sure the creaselines of the appliqué are exactly over the creaselines of the plain square.

Pin and baste the appliqué piece in position. Baste it to the plain square through all the creaselines. Make smaller basting stitches ¼" inside all the cut edges of the appliqué. This is important because it holds the appliqué down during the somewhat rigorous and time-consuming stitching (Figure 4).

The appliqué is now stitched to the background. This can be done by tiny hand stitches or with the machine overcast. I like both methods of stitching. The hand stitching is very relaxing to do, and it looks soft and fine. The machine work is not necessarily faster because of all the curves and tying of ends that must be done. It has a more graphic look than the hand stitching.

If you are working by hand, thread your needle in a color to match the appliqué. The raw edges of the appliqué are tucked under as you work. Use the point and shaft of the needle to coax under about ⅛" of the fabric. This doesn't require clipping the edge because you are turning under such a tiny amount. Don't give up quickly. This may take some time to learn. Go slowly, and put your feet up somewhere. Take as small a stitch as you can, don't rush it (Figure 5).

If you can't stand hand sewing, or you just like machine embroidery better, work a satin stitch directly over the raw edge of the appliqué. Adjust your machine to a medium-width zigzag with very close stitches. Follow the shaped edge of the appliqué. Make the curves smooth and the points sharp. Tie the ends of your thread when you stop stitching. Try making the machine stitching in a third color.

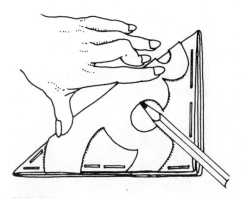

FIGURE 3:
Drawing around the pattern on the fabric

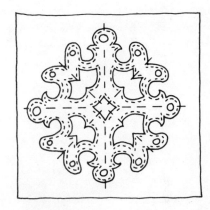

FIGURE 4:
Basting the appliqué to the background piece

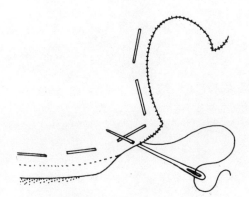

FIGURE 5:
The tiny overhand stitches used to finish the edge of the appliqué

FIGURE 6:
The appliqué with echo quilting

Quilting the block:

Prepare the block for quilting as shown in Block 1, Figures 1 and 2. The piece can be quilted by hand or by machine. Draw a quilting diagram directly on the fabric. Follow the outline of the appliquéd piece using the technique of echo quilting. See Block 1, Figure 3A, for an explanation of echo quilting.

Make the rows of quilting as close together as you like. Many rows of closely-spaced quilting look very good with this technique. The background as well as the appliqué piece can be quilted (Figure 6).

The block is now ready to use for the Perky Picnic Pack in the next part of this chapter. Or it would be perfect for any other project as well.

The block can also be used in the unquilted form for projects that require an unquilted block. Try reversing your color scheme for a second block. This would make a positive-negative version of the design.

$\left(\begin{array}{c}\textit{Project} \\ \textit{10}\end{array}\right)$ # A Perky Picnic Pack

This project uses *one* sample block. It should be quilted. The block is used as a decorative center for a folding, portable picnic kit. The kit holds everything you need for a picnic for four except the goodies. Flatten it out and the places are already set!

SUPPLIES

One sample block, quilted or unquilted

1 yard of gingham

> Get one-inch-checked gingham in red. You could use any printed fabric.

3¾ yards of 44"-45" wide solid medium-weight fabric

> This is for the backing and the main construction of the project. Choose a color that accents the gingham or printed fabric.

1½ yards of 1½" to 2" wide webbing

> This is for the two handles. If you can't find a color you like, you can make the handles from the solid fabric.

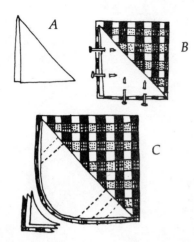

FIGURE 7:
Making the pockets
in the gingham squares

5 yards of 1″ wide bias tape
>Get bias tape in a contrasting color to bind the outer edges.

1½ yards of ¼″ wide elastic
>You need this for the elasticized pockets.

Thread
>Get one spool to match the solid fabric and one to match the bias tape.

DIRECTIONS

Cutting:

Cut four 15″ squares from the gingham or printed fabric. Cut the following pieces from the solid fabric:

eight 15″ x 15″ (assembly squares)
one 43″ x 43″ (base piece)
three 10″ x 25″ (elasticized pockets)
eight 2″ x 12″ (ties)

Assembling the four place settings:

The triangles in each corner of the Picnic Pack are made to hold a paper plate, napkin, and plastic utensils. Fold four of the solid color squares in half diagonally. Press them flat with the raw edges matched forming a triangle (Figure 7A).

Put one solid triangle on the right side of each gingham square. Match the raw edges on two sides. Pin and baste the triangle to the gingham (Figure 7B).

Find the center of the folded edge of the solid triangle. Press a diagonal crease on the triangle and gingham square. A paper plate is 9″ to 10″ in diameter. Our plate pocket is 10½″ wide. Measure 5¼″ out from the center on both sides of the triangle. Draw a line parallel on each side that is 5¼″ away from the center crease. Machine stitch the triangle to the gingham on the line. Secure the end of the stitching well at the diagonal fold by backtracking. Make a second parallel row of stitching 1″ outside the first row on both sides. This forms a pocket for the fork on the left and the knife on the right.

Make a third parallel row of stitching 1″ to the right of the knife pocket. This forms a pocket for the spoon (Figure 7C).

Round the corner that forms the bottom of the plate pocket. Use a small plate to draw a smooth, round edge as shown in Project 7, Figure 6. Cut the corner off on the line (Figure 7C). Baste all the layers together at the new rounded corners.

Elasticized pockets:

Make three elasticized pockets from the 10″ x 25″ pieces. See Project 9, Figure 20, for instructions on making an elasticized pocket. Cut your elastic into three 15″ pieces. Do *not* press under the side edges of the pockets before you gather the bottom of the pocket. Leave the side edges raw. Gather the bottom edge of the pocket to 15″ long. Each pocket is sewn to a solid color 15″ square. Match the side and bottom raw edges of each pocket to three raw edges of each square. Pin and baste the pocket in place (Figure 8).

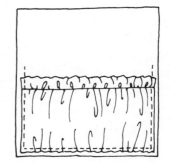

FIGURE 8:
Construction of the elasticized pockets

The ties and one handle:

Cut one 22″ piece of the webbing for the handle. If you have decided to make your handles to match from the solid fabric, see Project 3, Figure 15, for instructions.

Position one handle on the remaining 15″ solid square. The sides of the handle should be 3½″ from the sides of the square. See Project 3, Figure 16, for instructions on handle placement. Pin the handle to the center of the square.

Make eight ties from the 2″ x 12″ pieces. Instructions for making ties from fabric are given in Project 1, Figures 13 and 14. Turn back ½″ on only *one* end of each tie. The other end will be left raw. Topstitch the ties if you like.

Position two ties opposite the handle on the plain solid square. They each should be 3½″ from the sides of the square. Match the raw edges and baste the ties in place. Pin the ends of the ties to the square so they don't move around. See Project 5, Figure 3B, for positioning ties.

Put two ties on the side edge of one of the elasticized pocket squares. The ties are each 3½″ from the side corners of the square. One of the ties will be basted on the edge of the pocket and one will be on the square (Figure 9). Pin the ends of the ties to the center of the block.

Put one tie on each side of the handle on the plain square. The sides of the tie should touch the sides of the handle. Put the remaining two ties on the top of one of the elasticized pocket squares. They should be 3″ in from the upper corners of the plain square (Figure 9).

Assembling the blocks:

Lay the nine blocks of the Picnic Pack out as shown in Figure 9. Make sure all the blocks are turned in the right direction. The sample block is in the center. Stitch the blocks together using a ½″ seam allowance. Match the corners of the blocks where they intersect. See Block 2, Figures 3 and 4, for the method of stitching squares together. Press the seams open. Trim the seam allowances diagonally where they intersect, to eliminate bulk.

After the blocks are joined, they are sewn to the base piece. Put the 43″ base square flat on the floor with the right side against the floor. Position the joined blocks, right sides up, on top of the base square. Match all the raw edges. Make sure both pieces are smooth and flat.

Round the corners of the base square to match the corners of the nine-block section. Pin and baste the raw edges together. Pin and machine stitch the two pieces together directly on top of the seams of the nine squares. You will be stitching a large tic-tac-toe design. This stitching secures the two pieces together and makes them easy to fold.

Apply bias tape to the outer raw edges of the Picnic Pack. See Project 7, Figure 8, for two methods of applying bias binding.

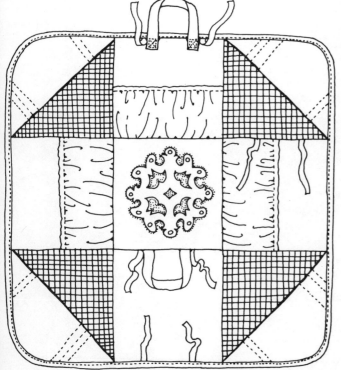

FIGURE 9:
The placement of all the squares on the pack

The other handle:

Cut a 26″ piece of webbing for the second handle. Press under ½″ on both raw ends of the second 26″ handle piece. Position it opposite the first handle along the edge of the elasticized pocket square (Figure 9). The ends of the handle should extend onto the Picnic Pack for about 2″. See Project 4, Figure 10, for instructions on how to sew the handle in place.

Folding the Picnic Pack:

Put the Picnic Pack on the table with the right side down and the handle at the top. Fold the right side of the Pack over the center section. Fill this with plates, napkins, etcetera (Figure 10A). Next fold the left section on top of the right section. Fill it with plastic forks, spoons, etcetera (Figure 10B). Fold the bottom squares over the center squares. Tie the ties to hold the squares in position (Figure 10C).

Fold the Pack so that the handles are together. The sample block will be on the outside of the Pack. Tie the top edges together at the handles. There is an elasticized pocket on the back of the folded Pack for paper cups and any light items that are not flat.

SUGGESTIONS

The Perky Picnic Pack is the perfect way to organize your next lunch in the park. Choose a sample block that will make a good centerpiece. Everyone always stops me to comment on my bag when I carry my pack in the park. Use several bright fabrics that go together well and make a cheery tablecloth. Don't worry about putting it on the ground because the whole thing goes right into the washer when you get home. I guarantee your dinner guests will be amazed when you open up your table setting on the grass!

SIMPLIFICATION

Elasticized pockets: To save time, you can eliminate two of the elasticized pockets. The one on the block with the handle is really handy for carrying paper cups so it would be better not to omit that one.

Ties: The ties can be made from bias tape rather than from fabric if you like. These are quicker and they will match the bound edge of the pack. See Project 7, Figure 8A, for the instructions.

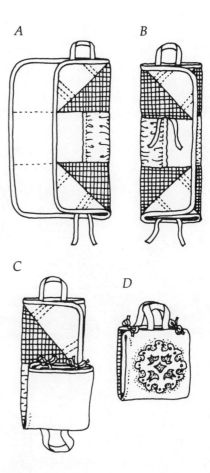

FIGURE 10:
Folding directions for the pack

CHAPTER ELEVEN

Block 11 Corded Quilting

This technique qualifies as quilting because it is made from two layers of fabric and a filler. The difference between this and regular quilting is that the filler is added *after* the stitch design has been made.

Linear designs work best for this technique. The stitching is done through two layers, the top and the backing fabric. Close parallel rows of stitching are made about ¼" apart. The entire design is stitched in this manner by hand or machine. These channels are then filled by inserting lengths of yarn from the wrong side. When the work is completed, the yarn plumps out the channels. By varying the width of the channels, you can make a sharp, precise, and well-defined design. Letters are easy to do with this technique.

A loosely woven fabric is necessary for the backing fabric. An average grade of muslin is fine. Depending on your design, the top fabric can be almost anything. If you use a knit or stretch fabric on top, the filler can really expand the channels, creating a very high relief surface. Each fabric should be tested individually to determine how well suited it is for this technique.

For this block, select a bright color of medium-weight fabric. This is for the background of the block.

Any name can be written on the life preserver, your own or your yacht's! An entire alphabet is included so you can spell the name out yourself. The letters are stitched and stuffed using the corded quilting technique.

SUPPLIES (enough for one sample block)

½ yard of a bright color of fabric
>This is for the background of the block.

½ yard of white cotton knit fabric
>This knit is for the life preserver.

½ yard of muslin

One 2 ounce skein of white four-ply knitting worsted
>This yarn is used to fill the stitched channels. It should be the same color or a lighter color than the fabric it will be stuffing. If it is darker, it will show through the fabric.

2 yards of white ½″ rope-like cotton cording

Piping
>Select a third color that accents the white knit and background color. If you are making your own piping, you will need ½ yard of fabric and 1½ yards of cotton cording. You need 1½ yards of piping.

Thread
>Match the color of the piping. It is for construction.

Embroidery floss
>For outlining the letters and the rope design. Select a contrasting color.

Polyester fluff
>A handful of stuffing about the size of a cantaloupe is needed to stuff the life preserver.

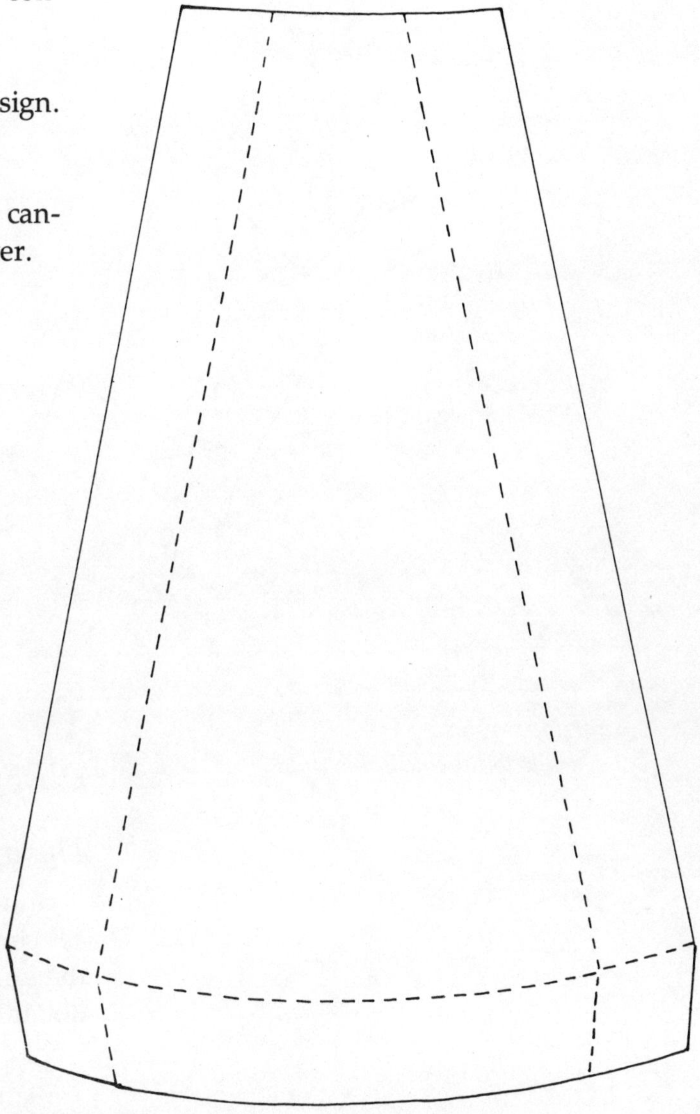

FIGURE 1:
The rope holder pattern

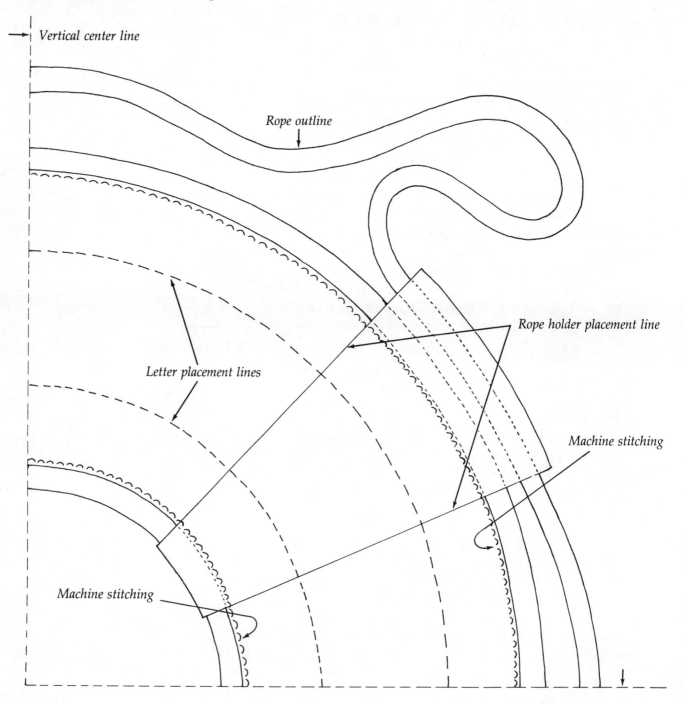

Vertical center line

Rope outline

Rope holder placement line

Letter placement lines

Machine stitching

Machine stitching

Horizontal center line

FIGURE 2:
A guide to the finished layout

DIRECTIONS

The life preserver pattern:

Draw a 3½" circle on a large piece of paper. Draw a 12" circle around the 3½" circle so that they both have the same center. Cut on both lines. Do not cut into the doughnut shape pattern.

Use this pattern to cut one doughnut shape from the muslin and the knit fabric for the life preserver.

Figure 1 is a pattern for the rope holders on the life preserver. Transfer this pattern to paper. Cut four rope holders from the same fabric as for the life preserver.

Figure 2 is a guide for the layout of one-quarter of the life preserver. Transfer this to a large piece of plain paper folded into fourths. Trace the design onto one of the quarters of the folded paper. Follow the instructions for transferring by burnishing given under Adapting, Enlarging, and Transferring Your Designs (p. 25).

This guide is a drawing of the finished design. Seam allowances are not shown. Use this pattern as a *guide* only for the placement of the four rope holders and cotton cording.

Applying piping to the life preserver:

Put the wrong side of the life preserver piece on top of the muslin. Match the raw edges along the inner and outer circles. Both pieces should be smooth and flat. Baste the raw edges together (Figure 3).

If you plan to make your own piping, consult Easy Sewing Fundamentals to Master in Part One of the book (p. 36). Make 1½ yards of piping.

The outer circle and the inner circle of the life preserver are piped. Refer to Project 2, Figure 7, and Project 4, Figure 7, for instructions on applying piping. The ends of the piping are pieced as shown in Project 2, Figure 8.

Apply the piping with the zipper foot to the outer edge of the life preserver. Use a ½" seam allowance. Notch and press all the seam allowances to the wrong side of the life preserver. They should lie flat and not be seen at all from the front of the life preserver.

Next, put piping around the inside circle. After the piping is sewn around the inner circle, the seam allowance must be clipped every ½". Don't clip into your stitching. This allows all the seam allowances to be pressed flat on the wrong side of the life preserver.

The rope holders:

Press under the ½" seam allowance on the two long sides of each rope holder. Working from the right side, edgestitch these sides ⅛" from the crease. Use the thread that matches the piping (Figure 4) Trim the seam allowance down to ⅛" from the edgestitching.

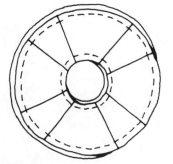

FIGURE 3:
Joining the two circles for the life preservers

FIGURE 4:

Folding in the seam allowances, and stitching the rope holders

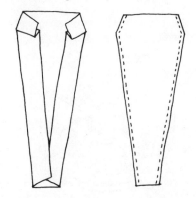

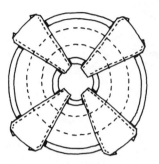

FIGURE 5:
*Positioning the rope holders,
and the letter placement lines
basted in place*

FIGURE 6:
*Placement of the letters
around the life preserver*

Transfer the rope holder lines from the pattern that you made from Figure 2 to the life preserver. Baste each rope holder in the correct position. The seam allowances will extend beyond the placement lines inside and outside the life preserver. Use the hand slipstitch to sew the top stitched sides down to the life preserver invisibly (Figure 5). Stitch only between the two circles of piping.

The lettering:

Transfer the two dotted circles on the guide to the *muslin* side of the life preserver. These are the placement lines for the letters. Baste along the lines so that they can be followed on the right side of the life preserver (Figure 6). The letters are placed between these two basting lines.

Turn the life preserver so that the line marked "vertical center line" is directed up and down. Trace the letters that you need for your name to a paper pattern.

Cut the letters out carefully. Space them out evenly on the life preserver according to the number of letters in your name. When the life preserver is in the vertical position, four letters will fit between the rope holders. Put two letters on each side of the vertical center line.

If your name is longer than four letters, put the four letters in the middle of your name between the rope holders. Put one letter in the center of each rope holder. Position any remaining letters equally on the basting lines outside the rope holders. If your name is very long, or you are doing several names, put the letters around the entire life preserver. It will hold up to sixteen letters. Tilt the letters slightly as you go around the circle so they look upright.

Place the letters around the right side of the life preserver as you want them. Draw a light pencil outline around each letter. After all the letters are traced, they are embroidered over the traced lines with a small backstitch. Use three strands of a contrasting color of embroidery thread.

Cord quilting the letters:

After it has been embroidered, each letter is filled with yarn from the muslin side. The yarn swells each letter up so it looks quilted on the right side.

Thread a large-eyed needle with two 24″ lengths of yarn. Pull the ends of the yarn so they are even. The Corded Quilting is done with four strands of yarn. Do not knot the ends of the yarn.

Insert the needle vertically into one of the letters just inside the back stitching. Do not go through to the right side of the life preserver. Pick up *only* the *muslin* so that the needle is between the muslin and the life preserver fabric (Figire 7A). Pull the yarn through the letter, leaving a ½″ end where you inserted the needle.

Insert the needle into the muslin in the same way about 1/16″ to the right of where the first stitch ended. Cross the entire letter between the layers. Do not pull the yarn tight. Emerge just inside the outlining stitches of the letter. A tiny loop of yarn is left along the edge of the letter. Continue working across the letter like this (Figure 7B). Check the right side to be sure that the yarn is filling the letters well. If they look too flat, change to a puffier yarn, or use more strands.

Figure 7C shows how the completed letters will look from the muslin side. Figure 7D gives you an idea of how the rows of yarn look inside each letter.

Appliqué the life preserver to the background square:

Press under ½″ on the outer raw edges of the rope holders. Tuck the inner raw edge of the rope holders under the piping. Baste it to the muslin side. Cut a 15″ square from the muslin and the backing fabric. Baste them together along the raw edges.

Center the completed life preserver on the right side of the background square. Pin and baste it flat along the inner piped circle. Baste right over the rope holders next to the piping. Use a zipper foot and contrasting thread to stitch on top of the basting. Your stitching should be ⅛″ inside the piping. See Figure 2 for the stitching placement.

Lift the outer edge of the life preserver. It is lightly stuffed with polyester fluff. Distribute the fluff around the stitched inner circle underneath the life preserver. Pin the outer piped edge of the life preserver to the backing square. You will be encasing the stuffing inside. If the block won't lie flat, you have overstuffed it. When

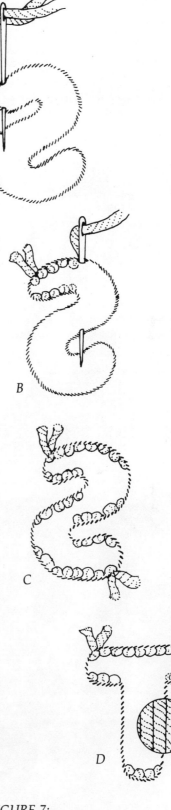

FIGURE 7:
Cord quilting the letters
from the muslin side
of the life preserver

FIGURE 8:
Pattern for alphabet letters

you have the right amount of stuffing under the life preserver, baste and machine stitch the outer piped edge as you did the inner piped circle.

The life preserver ropes:

Flip the outer loose ends of the rope holders in toward the life preserver. Pin them to keep them out of your way while working on the rope. Transfer the rope design from the pattern to the right side of the background square. The design continues right under the areas where the rope holders will be flipped over.

Begin applying the cotton cording to the backing square at a point in the middle of one of the rope holders, ¼" outside the piping. The cording will begin and end at this point. The raw ends will be butted and hidden by the rope holder when it is flipped over and stitched in place.

Use the whipstitch to sew the cotton cording to the backing square. Work on a flat surface. Position the cording over the design lines that you have transferred for a few inches. Stitch the cording in place. Lay out a few more inches of cording and stitch it down. Work in this way around the entire block until you reach the point where you started. Cut the cording and butt the raw ends. Secure them together with a few hand stitches.

Flip the rope holders over into their correct positions. They should cover the piping and the cotton cording. The outermost end of each rope holder is turned under ½". Slipstitch these ends in place to the backing square. They will extend ¼" outside the cotton cording (Figure 2).

This completes the sample block. Use it for any project in the book and especially for the Beach Blanket Bundle. The block makes a pillow that is also a pocket for carrying a towel.

SUGGESTIONS

This technique, like many of the others, can be used to decorate existing garments. But your initials on a T-shirt, or add a curlicue design to the hem of your old jeans.

Check a macrame or rope-tying book for lots of great linear designs. This technique is a good way to interpret the tying illustrations. They make beautiful designs.

Project
11

A Beach Blanket Bundle

This project uses *one* block. The block is used as the pillow section of beach rollup. This is a beach towel/bag all rolled into one. There are pockets for all the little things you need. You can't forget anything anymore because it all stows away together in one organized place until you head for the beach again!

SUPPLIES

One quilted or unquilted sample block
1 yard each of two different colors of terry cloth
These are for the blocks on the main part of the bundle.

2½ yards of medium-weight solid fabric

> This is for four pockets and the backing of the bundle that would lie against the sand. It shows when the bundle is folded up and should match the terry cloth. You might consider a waterproof fabric if it is not too stiff.

½ yard of medium weight fabric in a second color

> This is for the other four pockets so it should match the second color terry cloth.

12 yards of 1″ wide bias tape

> This is used for ties and to bind the edges. Pick out a color that goes with the terry cloth and the fabric.

1½ yards of 1½″ or 2″ wide webbing

> This is used for the handles.

Thread

> One spool to match each color of terry cloth and one to match the bias binding.

DIRECTIONS

Cutting:

The top of the bundle is made up of twelve terry cloth squares. There are two colors laid out in an alternate checkerboard plan. Cut six 15″ x 15″ squares from each of the two colors of terry cloth.

The pockets on the patchwork top of the bundle are cut from two different fabrics, the 2½ yards of backing fabric and the ½ yard piece. They are sewn on the terry cloth patchwork in an alternating color scheme. Eight pockets are needed. Cut four pocket pieces that measure 9″ x 10″ from each of the two fabrics.

Cut one 43″ x 57″ rectangle from the backing fabric. Also cut one 15″ x 16″ rectangle from this fabric. This is used to back the sample block pillow.

Making the pockets:

Make a hem in the top of each pocket as follows: Turn under ¼″ on the top edge of the pocket. Edgestitch this to the wrong side of the pocket. Fold down 1¼″ toward the right side. Pin and stitch this hem in place at both sides using a ½″ seam allowance (Figure 9A). Trim the seams and corners (Figure 9B). Turn the pocket hem right side out and press it flat (Figure 9C).

Round the two bottom corners of each pocket piece.

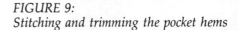

FIGURE 9:
Stitching and trimming the pocket hems

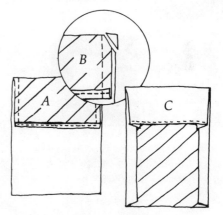

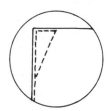

FIGURE 10:
Stitching the pocket corner for extra strength

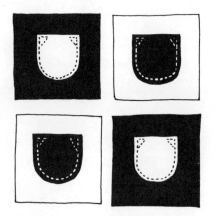

FIGURE 11:
Placing the pockets on the different colored terry cloth squares

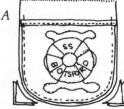

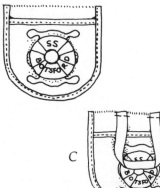

A

B

C

FIGURE 12:
Making the pocket/pillow from the sample block, and attaching the handle

Use a glass or small plate as shown in Project 7, Figure 6. The finished pocket measures 8" x 9". Press under the ½" seam allowance along the sides and bottom of each pocket. If you prefer square pockets to round bottom ones, make the pockets exactly as shown in Figure 9. Machine stitch ⅛" from the sides and bottom edges of the pocket. Make a triangle of stitching at the top corners of the pocket for extra strength (Figure 11).

Decide which color pockets you want to be sewn on each color of terry cloth. Position one pocket in the center of each of the terry cloth squares (Figure 11). You should have eight squares with pockets, four in each color of terry cloth. Pin and stitch each pocket in place as demonstrated in Figures 10 and 11.

The sample block pillow/pocket:

Decide which side of the sample block should be the top and mark it. Apply bias tape across the top raw edge of the block. See Project 7, Figure 8, for instructions on binding an edge with bias tape. Edgestitch the bias tape if it twists after applied.

Place the sample block on top of the 15" x 16" piece of backing fabric. Match the bottom corners of the block with the 15" side of the backing piece. The backing piece should extend 1½" above the sample block on the top side. Match the side and bottom raw edges. Round the two bottom corners of both pieces in the same way that you did the pockets (Figure 12A). Baste the raw edges together.

Bind the sides and bottom of the sample block and backing piece with bias tape (Figure 12B).

One of the handles for the bundle is put on the raw edge of the backing piece. If you want to make your own handles from fabric, see Project 3, Figure 15, for construction of a fabric handle.

Cut one 22" piece of webbing. Each end of the handle should be 3½" in from the sides of the backing piece. See Project 3, Figure 16, for a guide to the placement of handles.

Match the raw edges of one of the pieces of webbing to the raw edges of the backing piece. Baste it in place. Make sure it is not twisted (Figure 12C). Pin it to the center of the block so it doesn't move around.

Assembling the patchwork top section:

Lay the terry cloth squares out on the floor. Arrange them as shown in Figure 13. Stitch the terry cloth squares together with a ½″ seam allowance. See Block 2, Figure 4, for instructions on assembling squares. Make sure all the pocket openings are directed toward the top of the patchwork. Press the seams open. Trim the seam allowances where they intersect, to eliminate bulk. Round the four corners of the patchwork section by drawing around a small plate.

Ties:

The ties are made from bias tape. If you want to make your ties from matching fabric, refer to Project 1, Figure 14, for instructions.

Cut four 12″ pieces of bias tape. Press under ½″ on one end of each piece. Fold the bias tape in half lengthwise, and topstitch both sides. See Project 7, Figure 8, for an illustration on hemming and folding bias tape.

Put the raw end of one tie in the center of the raw edge of each terry cloth block on the left side of the bundle. Match the raw edges and baste them in place (Figure 13). Pin the ends of the ties down so they stay in place.

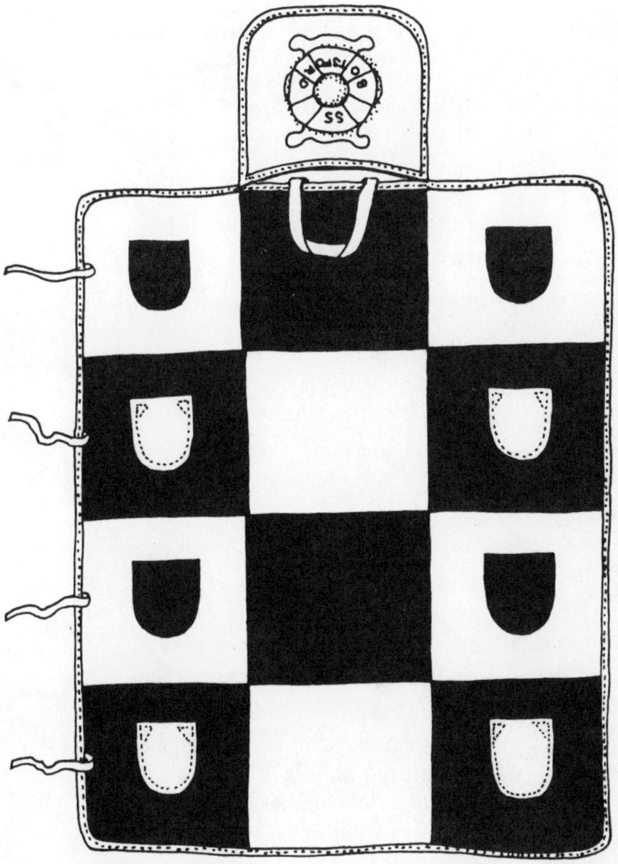

Attaching the backing piece:

Place the patchwork section on top of the 43″ x 57″ backing piece. The *wrong* sides should be together. Round the corners of the backing piece to match the terry cloth. Match, pin, and baste the two pieces together along all raw edges. Make sure the pieces are smooth and flat.

Pin and machine stitch the terry cloth section to the backing piece on top of the seams that join the terry cloth squares together. This will make a large twelve-square grid of stitching on the backing piece.

Attaching the patchwork section and the pocket/pillow:

Match the raw edge of the pillow section with the *center square* at the *top* of the patchwork section. The wrong side of the pillow section will be against the large backing piece. Baste it in place, securing the handle at the same time. Pin the pillow section to the patchwork

FIGURE 13:
The bundle showing the placement of the different squares

section so that it doesn't move around (Figure 14).

Apply bias tape to the entire outer raw edges of the patchwork section. You will be attaching the pillow section at the same time. Do not catch the bound edge of the sample block pocket into the bias binding.

Ties and one more handle:

Flip the bundle over so the backing piece is on top. Cut eight 12" pieces of bias tape. Hem both ends of each piece, fold them in half lengthwise, and topstitch them as you did before. Position one tie over the center of each stitching line on the left side. The ties should extend horizontally so they can be tied easily (Figure 15).

Position two ties on the top of the bottom block in the middle row. These ties should be vertical. Attach two ties on the top of the second block in the row on the right side. These ties should be vertical. These ties are each 3½" in from the corners of the stitched square (Figure 15). Sew these ties in place as shown in Project 1, Figure 15. Stitch through all the thicknesses of the bundle. The stitching will be almost invisible on the terry cloth side because of the loops of the terry.

Cut a 26" piece of webbing for the second handle. Press under ½" on each raw end. Position this handle on the bottom of the second square in the middle row (Figure 15). Stitch it in place as shown in Project 4, Figure 10.

Folding the Beach Blanket Bundle:

Put the Beach Blanket Bundle on the table with the right side up. Fill the pockets with whatever you plan to take along. Fold the right side over the center (Figure 16A). Fold the left side over the right side. Tie the ties, securing the edge in place (Figure 16B).

Fold the bottom square up over the next square. Fold both of these squares up together over the next square. Tie the ties (Figure 16C). Grasp both handles so that the bundle folds once again. The sample block pocket should flop down becoming the front of the bundle (Figure 16D).

SUGGESTIONS

The Beach Blanket Bundle is terrific for carrying all your things to and from the beach. You can put it right in the washer when it gets dirty or full of sun tan oil. You don't have to spread out a blanket on the beach anymore. You simply unfold it in its place. Everyone

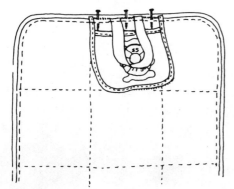

FIGURE 14:
Attaching the pocket/pillow to the terry cloth patchwork section

FIGURE 15:
The placement of the ties and the remaining handle on the back of the patchwork section

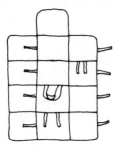

nearby always casts envious glances my way when I unfold my neat arrangement of pocketsfull of accessories. The corners of the bundle needn't be weighted down with sandals either! The contents of the pockets keep the corners flat. If you like you can attach bias tape loops at each corner. These can be wrapped around a wooden stake or a stone for extra hold. Tuck the handle into the pocket/pillow, out of your way.

SIMPLIFICATION

Pockets: You can eliminate all or a few of the pockets if you don't need them. The pockets can also be made smaller or larger if you like. However, if you are anything like me and my friends, you will need every pocket for all the junk that you cart to the beach!

FIGURE 16:
Folding instructions for the bundle

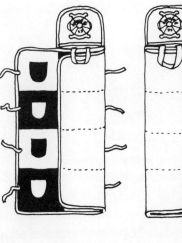

A   B   C   D

CHAPTER TWELVE

Block 12 · ## Stuffed Quilting

Stuffed quilting is a close cousin of corded quilting, described in the last chapter. The procedure is almost the same. Read through Block 11 if you are not familiar with the technique of corded quilting.

The top and backing fabrics are stitched together the same way as in corded quilting. The stitching design, however, does not need to be a linear one. It should be composed of shapes that create enclosed pockets, like circles, squares, or hearts. The two layers of fabric are stitched together along the design lines. This can be done by hand or machine.

After the design is completely sewn, the pockets formed by the stitching are stuffed. Only the pockets are filled. The background and remaining areas of the design are left flat. This creates a very decorative highly-raised surface. The stuffing is done from the wrong side by making a slit in the backing fabric. This method shows up best when done on light-colored fabrics.

Any variety of polyester fiber filling is an ideal stuffing. Be careful of substitutes for this sample block. Bits of old nylon stockings are fine as long as the color doesn't show through. Do not insert a colored filler such as yarn or fabric scraps into a white design. The colors of the stuffing will show through light-colored fabrics. The dyes in this type of stuffing might run when the block is laundered or dry cleaned.

For this sample block, satin is a good choice. It gives a bit and puffs up nicely when stuffed. The lustrous sheen shows off the stitched and stuffed designs really well. This is a fabric that may require dry cleaning to retain its quality.

Knits and some pile fabrics like velveteen and velour make up well with this technique. They may be a bit tricky to handle. Test a swatch of these fabrics to determine if they will wash well. Some do and some don't.

I have an absolutely superb sample block made from silk velvet that caused more than one temper tantrum when I was making it. Unless you are very adventuresome, it is a good idea to make a small, stuffed sample of a section of your design on any fabric that you're not absolutely sure of.

FIGURE 1:
The wreath pattern

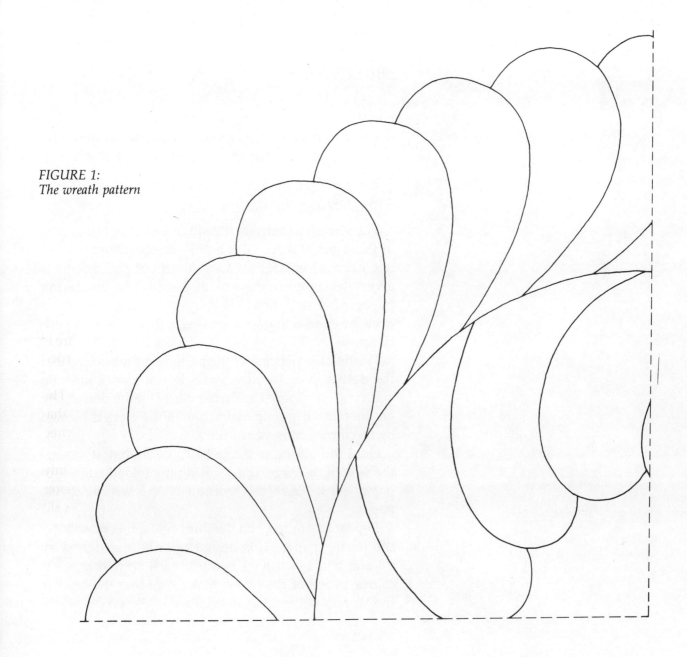

SUPPLIES *(for one sample block)*

½ yard solid color fabric
> This is for the top of the block.

½ yard muslin or white broadcloth
> This is the backing fabric.

Thread
> Pick a color that matches the top fabric closely.

Polyester fluff for stuffing
> This is sold by the bag; one bag will be plenty. You may have enough left over from another project; you need a ball of stuffing about the size of a basketball.

Tracing paper 18″ x 18″
> This is for transferring the pattern from the book. It can be plain or graphed.

DIRECTIONS

Cutting:

Cut a perfect 15″ x 15″ square from the muslin. Use this as a pattern to cut an identical square from the top fabric.

Transferring the design:

The wreath pattern for the stuffed quilting is included in this block (Figure 1). It is the correct size so you do not need to enlarge it. One-fourth of the design is given. To complete the wreath design, fold the tracing paper in half and then in half again. Open it out flat. Go over the intersecting, perpendicular fold lines with pencil lines.

Position the paper over the pattern in the book so that the dotted lines are directly under the pencil lines on your tracing paper. The corner made by the dotted line on the pattern should match one of the corners formed by the intersecting pencil lines.

Hold the tracing paper in place by folding it around the side of the page and securing the folded edge with paper clips. Trace this portion of the wreath to the paper.

Repeat this process on the three remaining quarters of the tracing paper. This design can't be transferred by folding and burnishing because each section is not a mirror image of the other. Make sure that the lines of the wreath pattern blend together at the points where they meet along the intersecting lines. You will match these lines each time you move the tracing paper.

When the wreath pattern is completely drawn, transfer it to your top fabric square. Fold the fabric into quarters as you did with the tracing paper. Use your iron to press the folds very, very, very lightly. Make only shallow creases that you can remove later by steaming. Use these shallow creases to center the tracing paper pattern on the fabric. Match the intersecting pencil lines to the foldlines in the fabric. Transfer the entire design to the right side of the fabric by one of the methods described in Adapting, Enlarging, and Transferring Your Designs (p. 36).

Stitching the design:

Position the top fabric square over the muslin square. The right side of the fabric with the transferred design centered on it should face up (Figure 2). Match the raw edges. Pin and baste them together ½" from the edges. Baste an X across the block from corner to corner. If you have chosen a very stretchy fabric, you may need to baste across the design in several directions. This prevents the top fabric from slipping and separating from the muslin during sewing.

Stitch directly on top of the transferred lines. Use the quilting stitch if you are sewing by hand. Make all knots on the muslin side (Figure 3).

Machine stitching will make this design sharper and more well defined. If you want to do it by machine, sew directly on the lines using a straight stitch. Set your machine so it makes about ten stitches per inch. Run the machine slowly so that you can make very smooth curves.

You will need to start and stop the machine stitching frequently. Do not go over a part of the design more than once. See Knotting the Ends of Your Threads, p. 38. This gives directions on securing thread ends in the center of your work. Cover the entire design with stitching. Remove the basted X.

Stuffing the design:

After all the lines have been stitched, you are ready to stuff the pockets. Working from the muslin side, carefully separate the muslin from the top fabric (now on the bottom) by pinching and pulling the fabric from below. Gently prick the muslin in the center of one of

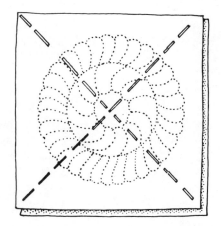

FIGURE 2:
Layering the fabrics, and transferring the wreath design to the top fabric

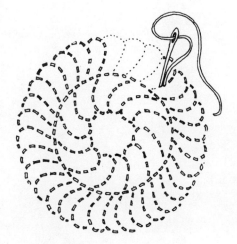

FIGURE 3:
Hand stitching the wreath design

the stitched pockets with your sharp-pointed embroidery scissors. Be *sure* that you do not catch the top fabric with your scissors.

Snip the muslin and make a tiny slash in the center of the pocket (Figure 4A). Take a piece of the polyester filler about the size of a cotton ball. Use a knitting needle or pointed metal nail file to push the filler into the pocket. Don't use a pencil! Avoid using any force; gently direct the filler into the corners of the pocket with the point of the needle or file (Figure 4B). You will be surprised how much filler it takes to fill one pocket. Look at the front to check your progress. Decide how tightly you want to pack the design. This will depend on what looks best for the type of fabric you have used. Stuff each pocket in the same way.

After each pocket is stuffed, you need to close the slash you have cut. The smaller the slash, the less sewing is necessary. Use small, loose stitches—just enough to keep the stuffing from escaping. You can close each pocket as you go or stitch them all at one time after they're stuffed (Figure 4C).

This block is now ready to use for the Traveling Treasure case in Project 12. It does *not* need to be quilted as described in Block 1.

This is a technique that can be used to decorate garments like T-shirts. Draw the design on the garment. Put a piece of muslin on the inside of the garment underneath the design. Stuff it from a slash in the muslin. The knit fabric of the T-shirt stretches a lot and makes an embossed design that is really decorative. Try stuffing the knees on children's overalls with the leaf-shaped design from Block 8!

FIGURE 4:
Slashing, stuffing, and closing the design from the muslin side

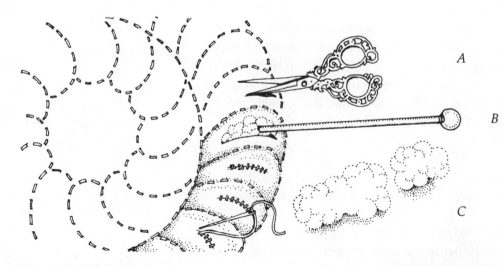

A

B

C

A Traveling Treasure Case

Project 12

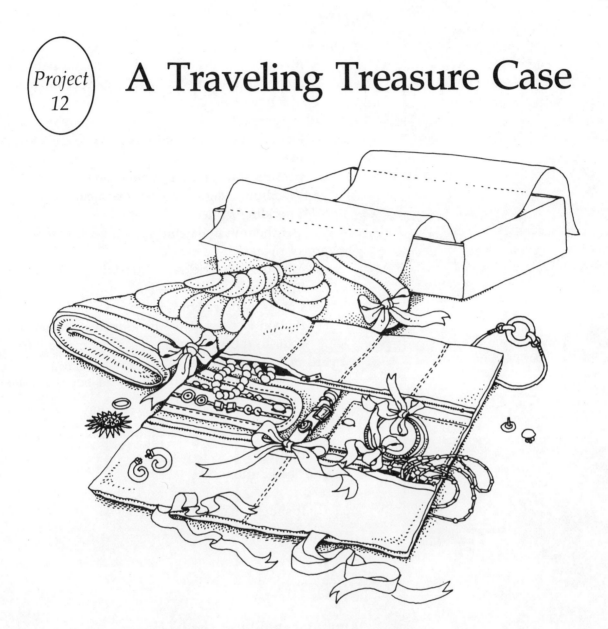

This jewelry case is made with *one* sample block. It should be quilted or composed of several layers of fabric so that the jewelry you keep inside is well protected. The block becomes the outside cover of the case. The wreath design shown in the Stuffed Quilting block is used to illustrate the construction of the case. Any sample block that is quilted could be used.

This project is great for traveling or just keeping your best jewelry safe and sound. The inside has several different sized pockets and compartments. There is a special stuffed holder for rings. Bangle bracelets and pierced earrings have their own specially designed places. Make it from almost any medium-weight fabric. Make it feminine or sophisticated, as a gift or for your own special "crown jewels."

SUPPLIES

One sample block
> It can be quilted or unquilted. Back a partially quilted or unquilted square with a second layer of fabric or fleece.

1 yard of fabric
> Pick a solid or printed color that blends with the block you are using. It is used to make the pockets and compartments inside the case.

¼ yard medium weight iron-on interfacing

two 14″ neckline zippers
> Get them in a matching or an accent color.

1 yard of rickrack
> Medium-sized rickrack. Match it to the color of the zippers.

3 yards of ½″ wide ribbon
> Ribbon is needed for tie closures. Match the color to the zippers.

1 yard of 1″ wide bias tape
> Bias tape is used to finish the edges of the pierced earring holder.

1¾ yards of ¼″ cotton cording
> You need cording for piping the outer edge of the case.

two ½″ ball buttons

Thread
> It should match the fabric.

DIRECTIONS

Applying piping to the block:

The sample block is bordered with piping to give it a nice firm edge. Cut bias strips from your own fabric to make matching piping. Follow the piping instructions given in Easy Sewing Fundamentals to Master, p. 36.

Apply the piping to the sample block as shown in Project 2, Figures 7 and 8.

Cutting:

Cut the following pieces from the fabric that is left after the piping has been made. The straight edges of the pieces should be parallel to the lengthwise or crosswise grain of the fabric.

one 15″ x 15″ base piece
two 5″ x 15″ pockets B and C
one 6″ x 15″ center piece
one 5″ x 8″ pocket A
three 1½″ x 6½″ pierced earring holder
one 2″ x 5″ stuffed ring holder

Making the ring holder:

The ring holder is a small fabric tube that is stuffed. It holds rings snugly when it is tied in place with its own ribbon tie. Rings slide on and off easily when you untie it.

Fold the 2″ x 5″ rectangle in half lengthwise with the right side inside. Mark a seamline ¼″ in from the long raw edge. Pin and stitch on this line (Figure 5A). Slip the stitched tube over a pencil. Spread the seam allowances open, and press them flat. The pencil prevents you from creasing the tube in half (Figure 5B).

Remove the pencil. Cut a 10″ length of ribbon. Slip it through the tube until it extends slightly out of the other end. The seam allowance in the tube should be centered over the wrong side of the ribbon. Match all the raw edges. Stitch across the end of the tube and the ribbon, securing them together ¼″ from the raw edge. Secure the ends well (Figure 5C).

Pull the ribbon out gently from the open end of the tube. The tube will turn right side out automatically (Figure 5D). Stuff the tube from the open end with any type of filler. Use a knitting needle to guide the filler into the tube. Pack the filler tightly. Leave about 1″ at the end of the tube unstuffed. Baste the end closed with the raw edges even.

Attaching the ring holder:

The ring holder is positioned on the 6″ x 15″ center piece. Fold the center piece in half crosswise and mark the center with a pin on both raw edges.

Cut a 10″ length of ribbon. Center it over one of the pins. The raw edge of the ribbon should be even with the fabric edge. Baste this in place ½″ from the raw edges (Figure 6A).

Place the raw edge of the ring holder at the center mark on the opposite edge. The seam of the ring holder should be face down. Baste this in place as you did the ribbon (Figure 6B).

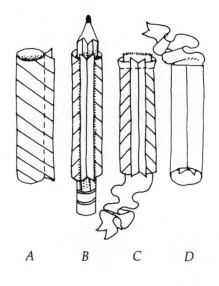

FIGURE 5:
Construction of the ring holder

A   B   C   D

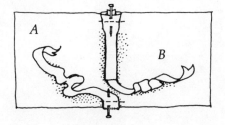

FIGURE 6:
Placement of the ribbon tie and ring holder

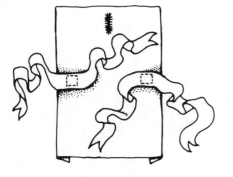

FIGURE 7:
*The ribbon ties on the pocket
for bracelets. The button hole*

FIGURE 8:
*Stitching pocket A
to the center piece*

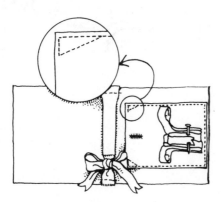

Making pocket A:

One of the shorter sides of the 5″ x 8″ pocket piece is to be hemmed. Follow the instructions for making a pocket hem in Project 11, Figure 9A, B, C. Leave the bottom edge of the pocket straight and unhemmed. Press under a ½″ seam allowance on the two long sides of the pocket.

Cut two 16″ lengths of ribbon. Fold each one in half and mark the center. Position them on pocket A so that the centers are 3″ away from the hem and ¾″ in from the finished edge. Sew them in place by stitching a small box on the ribbon (Figure 7).

Make a button hole in the center of the hemmed end of the pocket. The buttonhole should begin about ½″ from the folded edge of the hem. Make it long enough to fit one of the ½″ ball buttons (Figure 7).

Attaching pocket A:

Pull all the ends of the ribbons to the center of the pocket. Pin them in place so they are not in your way. Match the raw edge of the pocket to the raw edge of the center piece. The sides of the pocket should be 1″ from the top and bottom raw edges of the center piece (Figure 8).

Pin and stitch the pocket in place ⅛″ from the sides and raw edge. Make a triangle of stitching at the two top, hemmed, corners of the pocket. These corners of the pocket get heavy wear. This way of stitching prevents them from tearing out (Figure 8).

Sew one of the buttons to the center piece so that it will fit into the buttonhole.

Making the holder for pierced earrings:

This holder is the perfect way to keep all those tiny earrings from getting lost. It is an ingenious way to make your own earring organizer.

The three 1½″ x 6½″ strips need to be interfaced. Use the strips as a pattern to cut identical pieces from the iron-on interfacing. Fuse one piece of interfacing to the wrong side of each strip.

The rickrack is inserted between the strips. Beginning at the end on the *right* side, align the rickrack with the long side of one of the strips. The points of the rickrack should almost touch the raw edge (Figure 9A). Baste it in place.

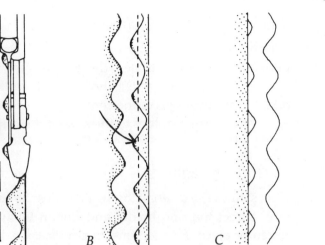
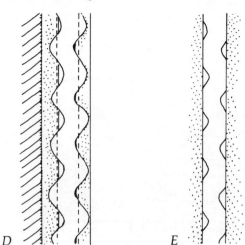

FIGURE 9: Construction of the earring holder

Put the zipper foot on your machine. Push the foot over so that it is on the right side of the needle. Stitch the rickrack down, catching only the outward points. Your stitching should pass very close to the inward curves of the rickrack, but it must *not* stitch over these curves (Figure 9B). These tiny openings are for inserting the earring posts.

Press the ¼" seam allowance to the wrong side. Notice the tiny openings that you have made along the fold (Figure 9C).

This strip is now ready to be joined to the second strip. Place the rickrack edge of the first strip against the edge of the second strip with the right sides together. Baste. Stitch the rickrack to the second strip in the same way you did before (Figure 9D). Press the seam allowance of the second strip back. You now have two strips with a channel of rickrack between them. Tiny alternating holes are created by the rickrack along the folds of both strips (Figure 9E). Make a second channel of rickrack with the third strip in the same way.

When the three strips are assembled, round one end of the two outside strips; draw around the end of a large spool of thread to get a good curve. Cut on the line you have drawn (Figure 10).

Bind the two long sides and the curved end with 1" wide bias tape (Figure 10). Instructions are given on most packages. If not, check Project 7, Figure 8, for the technique of applying bias tape.

Work a buttonhole to fit the other ½" ball button. Center it in the middle strip about ½" from the rounded end.

FIGURE 10:
Binding the earring holder
with bias tape

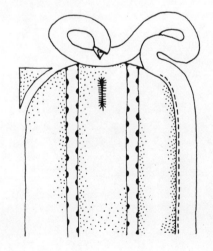

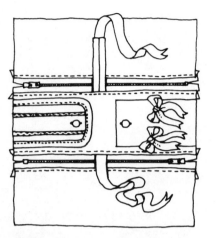

FIGURE 11:
Attaching the earring and bracelet holders,
the zippers, and pockets B and C

Attaching the earring holder:

Place the earring holder on the 6″ x 15″ center piece opposite the pocket. Match the raw edges. The side edges of the earring holder should be 1″ from the top and bottom raw edges of the center piece. Baste the raw edge of the earring holder to the side of the center piece (Figure 11).

Inserting the zippers:

Press under ½″ along both 15″ sides of the center piece. Direct the ring holder and ribbon tie away from the center piece. Position one zipper *under* each edge so that the center piece is about ¼″ from the zipper teeth.

The pull of one zipper is on one side of the center piece and the other one is on the opposite side (Figure 11). Baste the zipper tapes to the center piece ⅛″ from the edge. Use your zipper foot to stitch them by machine on top of the basting. Be careful not to catch the ring holder or ribbon tie in your stitching.

Overcast one 15″ edge of pocket pieces B and C. Press these edges under ½″. Tie the ring holder in place. Attach pockets B and C to the zippers in the same way you did on the center piece (Figure 11).

Making pocket dividers:

Put the 15″ base piece on the table with the right side up. Place the completed inside compartment section on top of the base piece with the right side up. Match the raw edges and baste them together.

Use the zipper foot to close off the top edge of the pocket. Stitch directly *on* the side of the zipper tape of both zippers that is closest to the center piece. This is the side of the zipper that was stitched first. The stitching will be as close to the edge of the center piece as possible (Figure 12).

Pocket B has two compartments. Mark the center of pocket B with a line. Beginning at the raw edge, stitch on the line toward the zipper. Stop at the edge of pocket B, make a square corner ¼″ away from the first row of stitching, and stitch back to the raw edge where you started. This divides pocket B into halves (Figure 12).

Pocket C has four compartments. Draw a line marking the center of pocket C. Draw a line on both sides of the center line that is 3¼″ from and parallel to the center line. This divides pocket C into four sections. Stitch on these three lines just as you did on pocket B (Figure 12).

The ribbon ties:

The jewelry case is folded or rolled and tied closed. Cut two pieces of ribbon that are 24″ long. Fold each piece so that it has one 8″ long end and one 16″ long end.

Put the fold in the ribbon on top of the left and right stitched dividers of pocket C. The shorter, 8″ end of ribbon should be underneath. Baste the two folds in place even with the raw edges of pocket C (Figure 12). Pin the ends of the ribbon ties to pocket C so that they don't get caught in the final seaming.

Assembling the case:

The compartment section is now stitched to the piped edge of the sample block. Put the sample block on top of the compartment section with the right sides together. Match the raw edges and baste the two pieces together. Leave an 8″ opening along the outer edge of pocket B.

Machine stitch the pieces together with a zipper foot. Sew as close to the piping as possible. Grade the corners and seam allowances to ¼″. Turn the case right side out through the 8″ opening. Press the case lightly. Close the opening with the even slipstitch.

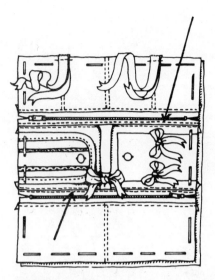

FIGURE 12:
Joining the compartment section
to the backing square,
and inserting the closure ties

SUGGESTIONS

The Traveling Treasure Case is a project that can't be simplified any further unless you change the design slightly. That's easy because this is what you have been doing throughout this book—redesigning and personalizing projects to meet your own needs.

This case could be easily adapted to hold things other than jewelry. Make it into a traveling sewing kit or a manicure set for a friend who is constantly traveling. By rearranging or customizing the pockets and ties, you can accommodate almost any type of small items. Make it from lightweight plastic for a cosmetic or a first aid kit. Use plaids and dark colors of fabric to make the case for a man.

SIMPLIFICATION

Ring and earring holders: These two parts of the case can be eliminated easily. They are very specialized parts of the case that many people wouldn't use. Make the case eliminating all references to these pieces. Put a pocket exactly like pocket A in place of the earring holder. It can be used for holding almost anything.

CHAPTER THIRTEEN

Block
13

Mock Smocking

This technique is one of my favorites. I've called it Mock Smocking because it resembles hand smocking. It is an organized pattern of folded and stitched fabric. It also has a springy elasticity similar to smocking. The design and texture of the fabric surface is very decorative. The series of intricate looking folds is surprisingly easy to do.

All of the stitching is done by machine. After measuring the correct intervals on the fabric, you sew vertical tucks in the fabric. These tucks are then twisted left and sewn with a horizontal row of stitching. In the next row, the tucks are twisted to the right. This twisting and stitching continues alternating left and right.

For this block, use broadcloth and a contrasting color of thread. After the stitching is completed, the block can be backed with a thin layer of batting. This gives the block the soft, dimensional appearance of quilting.

SUPPLIES (enough for one sample block)

½ yard solid color fabric

Use broadcloth or any medium weight fabric that can be folded easily. Avoid slippery or stiff fabrics.

Thread

Choose a contrasting color that will show up on the fabric well.

DIRECTIONS

Cutting:

Cut a 15″ x 21½″ rectangle from the solid fabric.

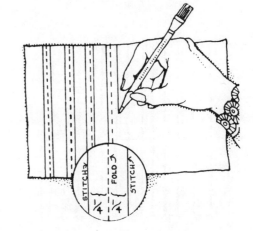

FIGURE 1:
Marking the fabric for the tucks

Making the vertical tucks:

There are thirteen ¼″ vertical tucks on the block. The space between vertical tucks is 1″. The tucks are made by folding and stitching on lines that you draw yourself on the right side of the fabric. Three lines are drawn parallel to each other. They are spaced ¼″ apart. The center line is the foldline. The other two lines are matched and stitched together.

Put the rectangle flat on a table. The 15″ sides should be vertical. Begin at the left edge. Draw a light chalk or pencil line that is 1½″ from the edge and parallel to it. Draw two more parallel lines to the right of the first one. They should be ¼″ apart. Be accurate; a slight error multiplies itself by thirteen tucks.

Draw a line that is 1″ away from the third line. This is the space between the tucks. It is also the first line of the next tuck. Draw two more lines spaced ¼″ apart. This completes the second tuck.

Continue drawing eleven more tucks in this manner across the rectangle (Figure 1). You will have drawn thirteen tucks altogether.

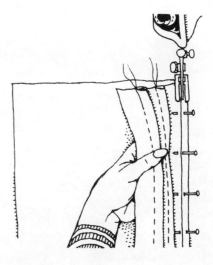

FIGURE 2:
Stitching the vertical tucks

Pin the tucks by folding on the center line, matching and stitching on the outer lines (Figure 2). Tie or reverse stitch both ends of each tuck. Continue stitching the tucks across the rectangle one at a time (Figure 3). After the tucks are completely sewn, the piece will measure 15″ square.

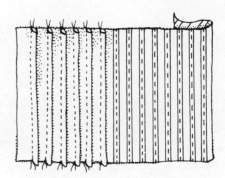

Making the twists in the tucks:

Pull the block out horizontally and press all the tucks to the right side. Make sure each tuck is pressed completely flat.

Draw a line across the top of the block that is 2½″ from and parallel to the top edge. Draw five more lines across the block that are spaced exactly 2″ apart. All the

FIGURE 3:
The block will become a square by stitching all the tucks

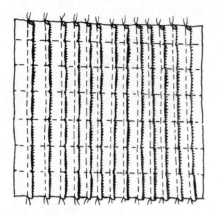

FIGURE 4:
Drawing the horizontal lines

lines should be parallel (Figure 4). There will be a 2½" space along the bottom of the block.

Stitch on each one of these horizontal lines, securing all the tucks to the right side. Draw a line 1½" from and parallel to the top raw edge. Draw an identical line at the bottom of the block. Draw lines inside each 2" space that divide the space in half. These lines are each spaced 1" from the stitched lines.

Stitch on these lines beginning at the right edge of the block. Flip each tuck over as you stitch up to it. Stitch the tuck in this position. This secures the tucks twisted to the left (Figure 5). Complete these alternate rows of stitching down the entire block (Figure 6). Press the block out flat.

The block is now ready to use for the Perfect Placemat in the second part of this chapter. It can be backed with batting and muslin for use as a quilted block.

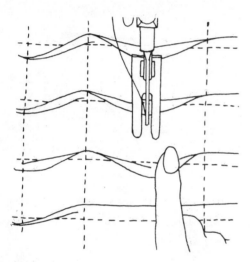

FIGURE 5:
*Twisting the tucks left and right
at 1" intervals*

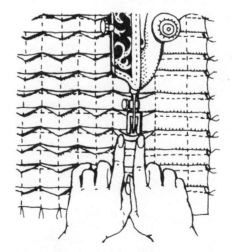

FIGURE 6:
*Twisting the vertical tucks
left and right*

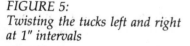

$\begin{pmatrix} Project \\ 13 \end{pmatrix}$ # A Perfect Placemat

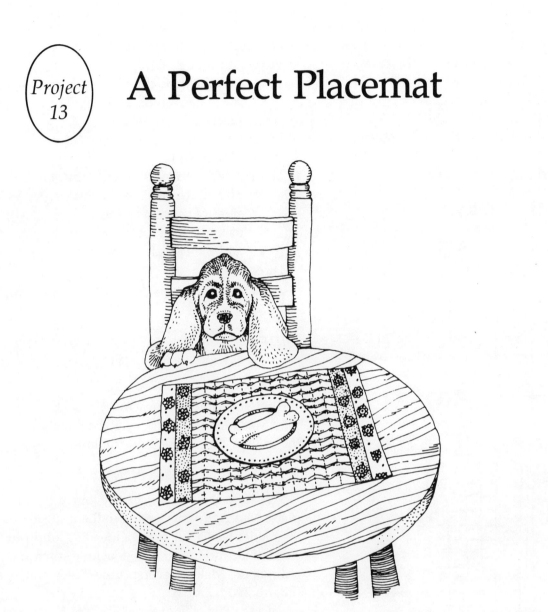

This project uses *one* sample block for each placemat that you want to make. The blocks should be unquilted. Strips of fabric are sewn to the sides of the block. The finished size of the placemat is 14″ x 18″. These strips can be made from one or several different materials. You can match the colors to your favorite dishes or use up some scraps leftover from another project.

   The entire placemat is then backed with a piece of thin batting or fleece and muslin. The placemat can be quilted if you like. The layer of filler provides padding to protect the table from heat. It also helps absorb spills.

SUPPLIES

One unquilted sample block

½ yard of lining fabric

> A solid broadcloth is fine. You may want to use the same fabric as one of the strips so the placemat is reversible.

½ yard of fleece

½ yard of muslin

⅛ yard each of two different fabrics

> These are for the patchwork strips on both sides of the sample block. They can be any type of fabric in colors that go well with each other and the sample block.

Thread

> It will be used for construction and quilting.

DIRECTIONS

Cutting:

Cut two strips that measure 2″ x 15″ from each piece of patchwork fabric. Cut one 15″ x 19″ rectangle each from the muslin, the fleece, and the lining.

Assembling the placemat:

Two different fabric strips are joined together into one piece. Match the edges and pin them together along one long side. Use a ½″ seam allowance, and put the right sides of the fabric together. Machine stitch and press the seam open. Make a second piece that is exactly the same (Figure 7A).

Decide what side of the block is to be the top. Pin one pair of strips on each side of the block. Put the same color or pattern strip next to the block on both sides. Machine stitch the seams and press them open (Figure 7B).

Quilting the placemat:

Prepare the block for quilting as shown in Block 1, Figures 1 and 2. Machine quilt on top of the seamlines that join the strips to each other and to the block. No additional quilting is necessary. The block can be quilted for a more decorative effect if you like. Some sample blocks will look like they need to be quilted and others won't. Make the decision yourself, and complete all the quilting at this point.

FIGURE 7

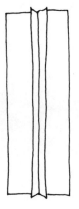

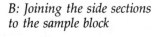

A: Seaming the two strips of fabric together

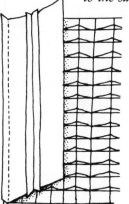

B: Joining the side sections to the sample block

Place the lining fabric on top of the right side of the placemat. Match the raw edges and pin them together as shown in Project 1, Figure 4. Leave a 6″ opening on one side to turn the placemat right side out. Trim the seams and corners to ¼″ as shown in Project 1, Figure 5.

Turn the placemat right side out through the opening. Gently push the corners out so they are pointed. Tuck the seam allowances in along the opening and use the even slipstitch to close it invisibly. Press lightly.

SUGGESTIONS

The placemat is probably one of the fastest projects to make. The quilting done on the sample block will involve the most time. You can quilt it by machine with just a few lines if you are making a placemat for every member of the family by suppertime tonight!

Rickrack or fringe can be sewn to the two sides of the placemat to make it a bit fancier. Any kind of trim could also be sewn around the entire placemat.

The construction of the placemat is the same as a simple pillow. The lining is the back of the pillow. Stuff the placemat before you close the opening. This is a good way to make "quickie" pillows from your sample blocks and scrap fabrics.

SIMPLIFICATIONS

Lining: If you do not want to line the placemat, the outer raw edges can be bound with bias tape. This really doesn't save any time; it just changes the look of the placemat by adding a solid color border. Some people may prefer applying bias tape to making a lining.

Fabric strips: One strip could be used rather than piecing two different fabrics together. Cut two strips that measure 3″ x 15″ and sew one to each side of the sample block.

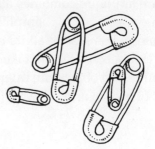

CHAPTER FOURTEEN

Picture Appliqué

Block 14

Picture appliqué combines all the appliqué techniques to tell a story or depict a scene. Each piece in the appliqué is a simplified representation of an object. It's like drawing a cartoon. This technique has a style all its own.

The subject can be taken from life, a photograph or a drawing. The shapes are simplified. Textures and objects are interpreted by fabrics. Brown corduroy is a good example. By varying the color of brown and the wale (the distance between the ridges) of the corduroy, it might accurately represent a log cabin, a plowed field, or even a corrugated cardboard box. Picture appliqué is more of a challenge than making simple appliqué designs because of the interpretations you will have to do. The pictures look equally well if they are done in a very realistic manner or merely suggest ideas in an abstract manner. The fabric, stitches, and techniques that you use are your decision to make.

For this block, I have included twelve different designs. "Which came first, the chicken or the egg?" You decide and select the one that appeals to you most. The pieces of each appliqué are drawn on fabric, backed with fabric fuser, and then fused to the background. The cut edges are then covered with hand embroidery stitches or a machine satin stitch. The eyes and the beaks are done by hand with embroidery floss.

Select fabrics to interpret the picture as closely as possible. Decide whether you will embroider the pieces down by hand or use the machine satin stitch. You can use the Stuffed Quilting technique to fill the shapes later if you like. The background in each picture could be quilted . . . or not. Muster up all the techniques you know and design your own block.

SUPPLIES (enough for one sample block)

½ yard of solid broadcloth

> This is for the background of the picture. Select a color that will show the appliqué off well. Sky blue or a neutral color is good.

Assorted scrap fabrics

> Find solid colors or small prints and textures. Designate each fabric for a particular piece of the appliqué. For example: yellow flannel is perfect for a baby chick with orange broadcloth for feet. White chintz makes a perfect eggshell!

1 yard of fabric fuser

Thread

> This will be used to appliqué the pieces to the background. Use matching colors or all black thread.

Embroidery floss

> Get one hank of each: black, white, medium blue, and orange.

DIRECTIONS

Enlarging the patterns:

The patterns have been printed as large as possible in the book. Select one or all of them for sample blocks. They need to be enlarged to about 10″ or 12″ in height so they will fit on a 14″ sample block. Refer to Adapting,

Enlarging, and Transferring Your Designs, p. 25. Use the grid method or an opaque projector to enlarge the design you have chosen. Draw a 14" square on your pattern paper, and make sure the enlarged design fits on it with at least a 1" border of background fabric on all sides. See the placement in the book.

Making the appliqué pieces:

After the design is enlarged, transfer each piece to a piece of the corresponding fabric. You can make templates or use one of the transferring techniques. Be sure to trace the patterns on the right side of the fabric. If you flip a pattern over and cut it out on the right side of the fabric, the piece will be reversed, the mirror-image of the original. These designs are not symmetrical; therefore, the pattern pieces must all be cut just as they are positioned in the original designs. Save your pattern to refer to later for placement.

After each piece of the design is drawn on the correct fabric, cut a square around each piece. Pin a piece of fabric fuser to the wrong side of the fabric. Baste the fabric and the fuser together inside the design lines. See Block 8, Figures 3 to 7, for an explanation on using fabric fuser for appliqué.

Cut out the appliqué pieces on the lines. You will be cutting the fuser at the same time. Position the pieces of the appliqué on the background square. Fit them together like a puzzle. Refer to the drawings in the book if you get confused about which piece goes where.

The hen's nests are cut out as *one* solid piece of fabric. Do not try to cut each piece of straw separately. If you would like some variation in the color of the straw, select a few scattered pieces of straw, trace them and make patterns. Cut these pieces of straw from another color and fuser. Appliqué them on top of the nest piece. This will give the impression of several different colored pieces of straw within the nest.

The lines on the nest that outline each separate piece of straw are done with hand or machine embroidery. Transfer the lines to the nest piece from the enlarged pattern. Cover each line with embroidery.

Stitching the appliqué:

After each piece of the picture has been fused in place, the raw edges are covered with stitching. Use the machine satin stitch or a hand embroidery stitch such as the outline or hand-done satin stitch. Cover all the raw edges and outlines of the design (Figure 1).

Embroidering the beaks and eyes:

The eyes are white with a blue center on the baby chicks. The hens and the rooster have black eyes. Use the outline stitch around the eyes to define them. Fill in between the outline stitch with the hand satin stitch. You could also use tiny blue or black buttons for the eyes.

FIGURE 1:
Stitching the raw edges
of each piece by hand
using a satin stitch
or an outline stitch

The beaks are all orange in a shade to match the fabric used for the feet. Work the outline stitch in black around the beak. Fill in with the orange satin stitch. Make a French knot for the nostrils.

The appliqué sample block is now ready to use. If you need a quilted sample block, it is very easy to quilt. Use the outline and echo quilting stitched around each design on the background fabric. It is not necessary to quilt the designs themselves. It would only get in the way of the embroidery.

These twelve patterns were designed especially for the Questioning Quilt project in this chapter. They can be used for any project in the book. Be certain that the placement of the pictures on the blocks is correct for the project that you are making. Be careful not to insert a tilted rooster on the Ace of an Apron or the Clever Clutch! In these two projects, the sample block is used diagonally.

The Picture Appliqué technique is perfect for decorating all types of items. Clothes and household things that have been bought are good subjects for spot decorations. Add an appliqué flower or animal to anything from jeans to your toaster cover. This is the perfect way to personalize everything without making it from scratch.

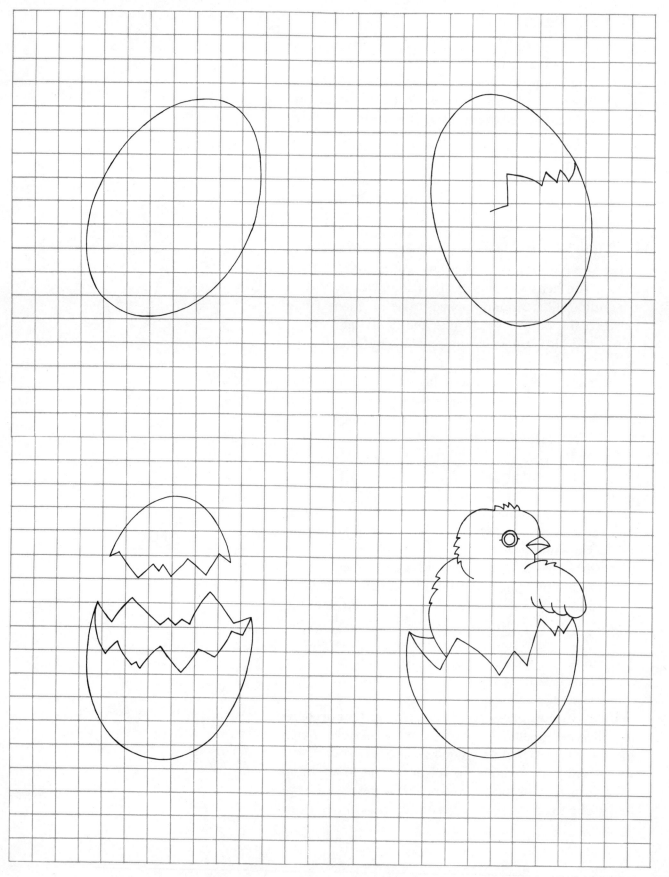

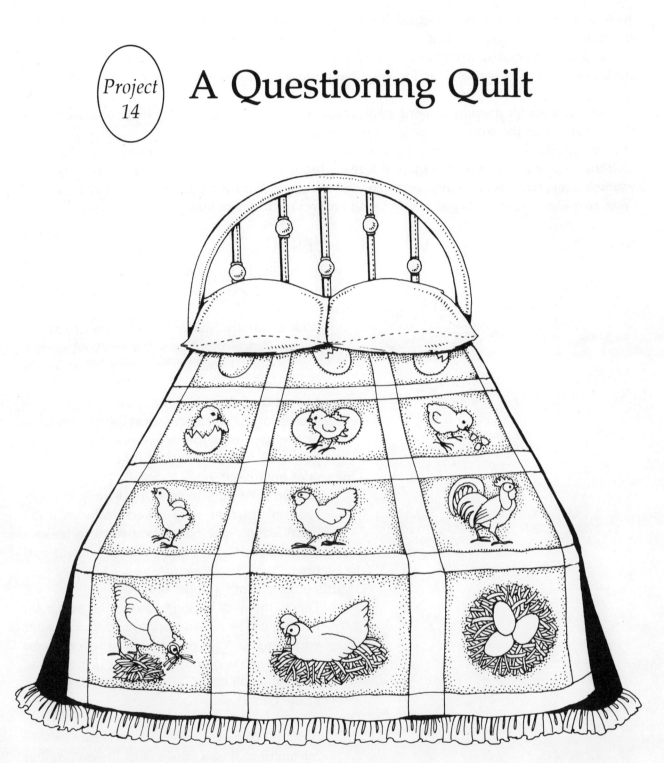

Project 14 # A Questioning Quilt

This project uses twelve blocks. You select them and lay the blocks of the quilt out however you like. The finished quilt measures 58″ x 76″. Patterns for the twelve squares of the Questioning Quilt have been given above, but use your favorite techniques to make each square, if you prefer.

This quilt is also an ideal way to use and display twelve of the sample blocks that you have made in previous chapters. Select twelve from your favorite chapters in this book and lay them out in any way that pleases you.

You can also make a pretty quilt by selecting one of the sample blocks and making all twelve blocks identical. The instructions for assembling the quilt are the same no matter which blocks you use.

Select colors for the narrow border and square corner pieces that will enhance and frame the blocks. Or match the color scheme in your bedroom.

Review all the techniques you have learned in this book and use them to help you design a quilt that is *your* idea of a perfect quilt. It is really fun to work on a project that you have designed yourself. Get going, get that quilt between your thimble and thumb right away. You've got lots of your own ideas right now; you needn't wait around for my next book!

SUPPLIES

Twelve unquilted sample blocks

2 yards of solid medium-weight fabric at least 44″ wide

> This is for the narrow borders between the blocks. Pick a color that will frame your sample blocks well. If your fabric is only 36″ wide, get three yards.

½ yard of solid medium-weight fabric

> This is for the small squares at the intersections of the narrow borders. Select something that goes well with the border fabric.

One roll of quilt batting

> The finished quilt is 58″ x 76″. Batting is packaged in different sizes. Check to be sure the piece is large enough. If you want to make a thick comforter, get two or three rolls of batting.

5 yards of broadcloth at least 44″ wide

> This is the quilt backing. It must be 44″ or 45″ wide. It can be a solid color or a print. Consider whether you want the quilt to be reversible or not. When a corner of the quilt is turned back, the lining will show. You could use a bedsheet in the correct size.

Thread

> Get the colors you need for construction and for quilting. If you plan to tuft the quilt rather than quilt it, get colored crochet cotton for the tufting.

DIRECTIONS

Cutting:

Make sure to straighten and square off all the fabrics. One crooked edge can throw the whole quilt off.

From the ½ yard of corner fabric, cut twenty pieces that measure 5″ x 5″. See Block 2, Figures 1 and 2, for quick methods of cutting small squares from fabric.

Cut thirty-one 5″ x 15″ rectangles from the 2 yards of border fabric.

Assembling the quilt top:

Lay the sample blocks out in the correct position. The quilt should have three blocks across the width and four lengthwise. You may want to number them so you don't get them mixed up. If the sample blocks have a directional design such as lettering or the chicken appliqués, make sure *all* the designs are placed right-side-up.

Begin with a 5″ corner square. Make a strip alternating squares and border pieces. There will be five squares and four border pieces in the strip (Figure 3). Make four strips that are identical. Use a ½″ seam allowance and press all the seams open. Be accurate and consistent with the ½″ seam allowance. If the seam allowances

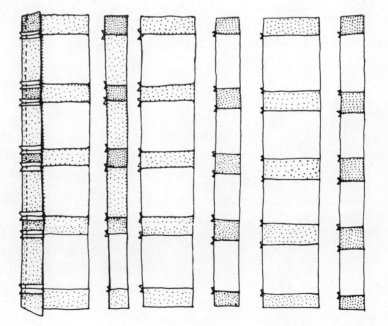

FIGURE 3:
Layout of the borders, corners, and sample blocks

vary or are uneven, the borders won't match exactly when the entire quilt top is sewn together.

Assemble the blocks in vertical strips with the borders. Begin and end with a border piece. Make sure all the sample blocks are upright and in order. Make strips with the next two rows of blocks in the same way.

Lay the strips out on the floor. Check the placement. A strip containing vertical borders and squares goes between each strip of sample blocks and also on both sides of the quilt top (Figure 3). Pin the strips together with lengthwise seams. Match all the seams where they intersect. Stitch each seam using a ½" seam allowance. Trim the seam allowances diagonally where they intersect to eliminate extra bulkiness. Press all the seams open.

Preparing the quilt backing:

Fold the 5 yard piece of backing fabric in half crosswise. You will have to divide it into two pieces approximately 90" long. Press a crease along the fold. Cut the piece in half along this crease.

With the right sides together, match the selvages of the two pieces. Remove the selvage from *one* edge of each piece by cutting about ¼" off the selvage edge. Cut both pieces at the same time. Pin these two trimmed edges together using a ½" seam allowance. Sew the two pieces together along this seam by machine. Press the seam open. This seam will run lengthwise on the back of the quilt.

If you are using a bedsheet, you will not have to make a seam in the backing. Make sure the sheet is large enough and includes seam allowances all around.

Assembling the three layers:

The quilt top, batting, and backing fabric are joined by smoothing each layer out on top of one another. This should be done whether you are tufting a comforter or quilting a quilt. Generally a quilt is thinner so the layers can be stitched together easily. A comforter is made of more than one layer of batting. This makes it difficult to stitch so it is tufted instead. It is much thicker and fluffier than most quilts. Tufting takes less time than quilting, but it doesn't have the refined, densely stitched appearance of a good quilt.

Enlist the help of a friend to spread the quilt out. It is hard to do it well by yourself. Besides, it is a moment for celebration. After all, you're finishing your quilt, and it's going to be beautiful!

Clear a place on the floor that is large enough to spread the quilt out flat. Take your shoes off because you will need to step on the quilt. Try not to work on a rug if possible. Put the seamed backing piece on the floor first. The *wrong* side should be up. Straighten it out until it lies perfectly flat. Weight the corners down with inverted coffee cups or canned goods. This keeps you from disturbing the backing fabric as you put the next layer in place.

Open the roll of batting and unfold all the creases in it. It helps to shake and fluff it gently. Hold one side and have your friend hold the opposite side. Carefully straighten out the batting and lower it onto the center of the backing piece. It will probably be smaller than the backing piece. Have an even border of the backing extending beyond the batting on all sides. If the batting is the same size or larger than the backing piece, match the raw edges or cut the batting down to the same size as the backing fabric.

Smooth out any bumps or unevenness in the batting. Weight it down on each corner. The batting should lie completely flat on the backing piece. If you want to use more than one layer of batting, spread additional layers out in the same manner. Baste the outer edges of all the layers of batting to the raw edge of the backing fabric.

Lower the quilt top with the right side up on top of the batting. Be careful not to disturb the smoothed-out batting. The top should be centered on the batting. Make sure it is absolutely flat. Remove any wrinkles by lifting and gently pulling the corners and edges.

When you are certain that all three layers are flat and smooth, pin them together. Begin in the center of the quilt. Pin through all thicknesses in radiating lines from the center point of the quilt. Baste the layers together on the pinlines. Begin basting at the center and work outward (Figure 4). Keep the quilt as flat on the floor as possible during the basting. Baste the raw edge of the quilt top to the batting and the backing on all sides.

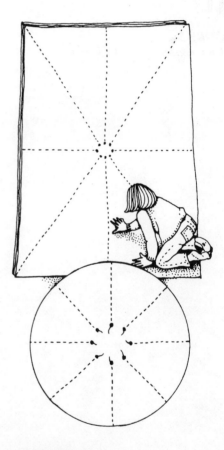

FIGURE 4:
Smoothing out the three layers of the quilt on the floor

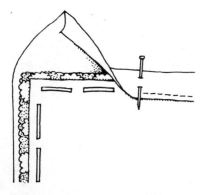

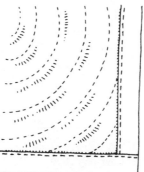

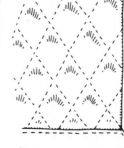

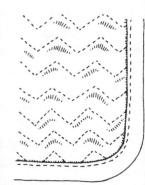

FIGURE 5:
A border made by the backing fabric

FIGURE 6:
Three corner suggestions

Finishing the edges:

The edges of a quilt can be finished in a number of different ways. Choose the method that will look best on your quilt. They should be finished *after* the quilt is quilted or tufted. I am explaining it now so that you will know how to trim down the batting and backing fabric.

The first method uses the backing fabric to make a border on the front side. Cut the backing fabric so that it extends 4″ beyond the raw edge of the top fabric. Cut the batting so it extends 1½″ beyond the raw edge of the quilt top.

Fold under a ½″ hem on all the raw edges of the quilt back. Wrap the backing to the front of the quilt. Cover ½″ of the raw edge of the quilt top with the hemmed edge of the quilt back. The edge can be sewn in place by hand or machine (Figure 5). The corners can be mitered or folded straight in place (Figure 6). The finished width of the border is 2″.

This method increases the length and width of the quilt by 4″ in each direction. You can vary the size of the border by just changing the cutting measurements.

In the second method, the two edges of the quilt top and back are hemmed evenly. Cut the edge of the backing fabric even with the raw edge of the quilt top. Trim the batting to ½″ inside both raw edges.

Fold the edge of the quilt back to ½″ over the batting. Baste this in place. Turn under ½″ on the quilt top so that it meets the hemmed edge of the backing. The edges can be stitched by machine or with the even slipstitch by hand (Figure 7).

Decorative trimming like lace, rickrack, or fringe can be inserted between the top and the backing before they are sewn together. This adds a decorative edge to the quilt. Baste the trim in place before sewing the edge closed (Figure 8).

Using method three, all three raw edges, top, batting, and backing, can be bound together with bias tape or a separate strip of fabric. See Project 7, Figure 8, for an explanation of bias bound edges.

Trim the batting and backing fabric even with the raw edge of the quilt top. Baste all the edges together. Apply the binding over all the raw edges (Figure 9).

Quilting:

If you plan to quilt the entire quilt top, the three layers must be basted together very well. Beginning at the center, make a basted grid over the entire quilt (Figure 10). This secures the layers together so they can be quilted easily. Careful basting also assures that the fullness of the fabric and the batting are evenly distributed. Any unevenness will be worked to the edge of the quilt by the basting. This prevents a tuck or pleat of fabric from forming because of extra fabric while you are quilting.

After the entire quilt is basted, draw the quilting diagram on the quilt top. See Block 1 for instructions on basic quilting.

This quilt construction is designed for hand quilting. Machine quilting such a large piece can be done. If you

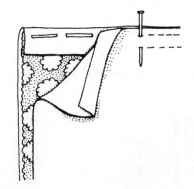

FIGURE 7:
Finishing the quilt by turning under the top and back evenly

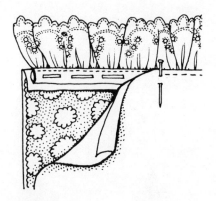

FIGURE 8:
Adding lace edging to the method in Figure 7

FIGURE 9:
Finishing the edge with binding or bias tape

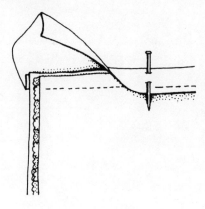

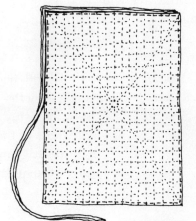

FIGURE 10:
A basted grid to prepare the quilt for quilting

FIGURE 11:
The locations for tufts

want to quilt by machine, work areas from the center of the quilt out to each side. Roll or fold up the side of the quilt you are not working on and pin it flat so that it can be passed through the open space of the machine to the right of the needle.

If you are quilting by hand, you may like to use a quilting frame. This is an oversized wooden frame that holds the quilt in place during stitching. It acts like a giant embroidery hoop, keeping the quilt taut while you're working. Unless you plan to make quilting a full-time hobby, I don't suggest you buy a frame.

The quilting can be done without a large frame. Make sure that the quilt is very well basted. Large circular quilting hoops are available in diameter sizes up to 30". They are much easier to use and to store than a quilting frame. You position the hoop over the areas to be quilted and move it as often as necessary.

After all the quilting is completed, finish the edges in the method you decided on previously.

Tufting:

This is a great way to make a wonderful, thick comforter. Use two to four layers of batting between the quilt top and back.

Yarn can be used for tufting; however, the best thing to use is a fine cotton cord like crochet cotton. It comes in lots of colors. Mark the places for each tuft with pins. They should be between 4" and 14" apart.

Make a tuft at each one of the corners of the squares in the border. Make two tufts in each narrow border piece along the seamline. They are spaced 7" apart.

The tufting keeps the layers of batting from snarling up inside the comforter. The more tufting you do, the more firm the comforter will be (Figure 11). See Easy Sewing Fundamentals to Master, p. 36, for instructions on tufting.

Finish the raw edges of the comforter after it is completely tufted. Any of the edge treatments would be suitable.

SUGGESTIONS AND SIMPLIFICATIONS

There are many ways to join the sample blocks together to make a quilt. You can use different sizes and types of borders between each block. Figure 12 shows two simple alternatives. Regardless of the way that you use, always sew the blocks together in strips first, and then sew the strips together.

The size of the borders will affect the finished size of the quilt. Make sure to check your mathematics carefully to determine the size of any quilt you design yourself. It is a good idea to sketch the quilt out carefully to the last detail so that you have a working drawing to follow and scribble notes on.

Some really fine quilts have been made from pre-quilted blocks. You might want to try it for assembling all those extra quilted sample blocks you've made.

The blocks are seamed together with the seam allowances on the quilt top. The seams are pressed open and trimmed to ¼". Bias tape or ribbon is appliquéd over the raw seam allowances on the top of the quilt.

Join the blocks into strips first, and appliqué the seams with ribbon. Next sew the strips together, and appliqué the long seams (Figure 13). Use 1" wide bias tape to bind the outer edges of the quilt. This is a fast way to assemble a quilt that allows you to quilt each sample block individually.

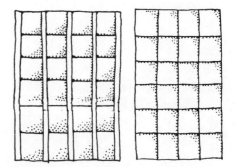

FIGURE 12:
*Suggestions for placement
of sample blocks*

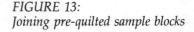

FIGURE 13:
Joining pre-quilted sample blocks

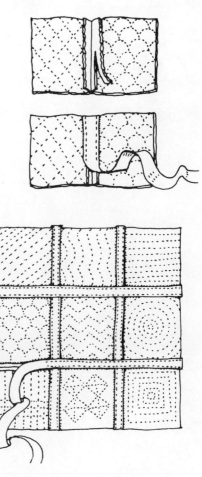

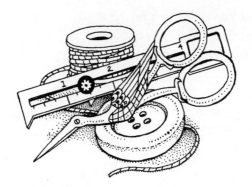

SUPPLIERS AND MANUFACTURERS

Most cities have at least one good fabric shop that has a wide selection of fabrics and notions. Large department stores generally have a fabric department, but it is usually not as delightful as the small fabric shop. Large stores are great for the standard assortment of things.

The small shop owner will generally have more variety in the choice of fabrics. You have a very good chance of discovering something special or unusual in the smaller store. There is also the added bonus of friendly sales people, a no-rush atmosphere, and possibly a few sewing hints when you need them.

Don't hesitate to ask for help. Question the fiber content of a fabric if you need to know what it is and if it isn't marked on the bolt. You also need to determine whether the fabric that you're buying is washable or must be dry cleaned. Some sales people are happy to give suggestions if you ask them. They can help you coordinate things; after all, they know their stock better than you do. They may have just what you're looking for tucked away in the back of the store. Some small shop owners might order something special for a good customer. I'm not suggesting that you make a pest out of yourself, just that you be a good, well-informed consumer.

Below is a list of some manufacturers that I suggest for their consistently fine-quality products. All the materials used in *Between Thimble and Thumb* are from these companies.

Fabrics

Crompton Company
1071 Avenue of the Americas
New York, New York 10018

Laura Ashley, Inc.
714 Madison Avenue
New York, New York 10021

Liberty of London, Inc.
229 East 60th Street
New York, New York 10022

Logantex, Inc.
1450 Broadway
New York, New York 10018

Souleiado at La Provence de Pierre Deux
353 Bleeker Street
New York, New York 10014

Springmaid by Springs Mills—Retail Fabrics
1430 Broadway
New York, New York 10018

Fabric fuser and interfacings:

Stacy Fabrics Corporation
469 Seventh Avenue
New York, New York 10018

Ribbons:

C. M. Offray and Son, Inc.
261 Madison Avenue
New York, New York 10016

Threads:

Coats and Clark's Sales Corporation
72 Cummings Point Road
Stamford, Connecticut 06902

Buttons:

Streamline Industries, Inc.
234-242 West 39th Street
New York, New York 10018

Zippers:

Talon Zippers distributed by Donahue Sales
41 East 51st Street
New York, New York 10022

Batting and fluff:

Stearns and Foster Company
Lockland
Cincinnati, Ohio 45215